CATHOLIC MOM 24/7
Daily Meditations for Busy Mothers

TAMMY BUNDY

ST. ANTHONY MESSENGER PRESS

Cincinnati, Ohio

Scripture citations are taken from the *New Revised Standard Version Bible,* copyright ©1989 by the Division of Christian Education of the National Council of Churches of Christ in the U.S.A. and used by permission.

Cover and book design by Mark Sullivan
Cover illustration by Christine Schneider

Library of Congress Cataloging-in-Publication Data

Bundy, Tammy M., 1961-
  Catholic mom 24/7 : daily meditations for busy mothers / by Tammy Bundy.
    p. cm.
  ISBN 0-86716-576-6 (alk. paper)
  1. Mothers--Prayer-books and devotions--English. 2. Mothers--Religious life. 3. Catholic Church--Prayer-books and devotions--English. 4. Devotional calendars. I. Title: Catholic mom twenty-four/seven. II. Title.
  BV4847B86 2003
  242'.6431--dc22

                                        2003022207

ISBN 0-86716-576-6
Copyright ©2004, Tammy Bundy
Published by St. Anthony Messenger Press
www.AmericanCatholic.org
Printed in the U.S.A.

Dedicated with love
to our Blessed Mother Mary.

INTRODUCTION

Read the Bible.

Pray more.

We know we should do these things. We know
they make us better people when we do. But as
with so many resolutions we make, we realize
our intentions and our time are not always
aligned.

We are moms. And whether we are balancing
fussy babies and nursing schedules or
balancing soccer practices and music lessons,
there just never seems to be enough time in
the day.

But still, we find ourselves longing for some
type of spiritual renewal. And it makes sense.
A mom cannot spend every hour of every
day—24/7—filling other people's needs

without running dry, unless she takes some time along the busy road to fill up for herself.

And so this book came to be. Just for you—a busy mom.

Each of the daily devotions begins with a Bible verse. I confess many of these were new to me. I'm embarrassed to admit I can recite every word of *Goodnight Moon* and *How the Grinch Stole Christmas*—and yet some of the most beautiful words of God that have been around for over 2000 years were unknown to me. Perhaps if they had come out on video featuring a dinosaur or some other type of animated character, I would have been more familiar with them.

But God doesn't work that way. He doesn't care about marketing potential or mass appeal. He doesn't show up as a figure in a Happy Meal. He just gives us His Words and waits for us to be ready to discover them. And that is what each day of this book begins with—a simple and yet beautiful Scripture verse that is waiting to be discovered.

After each verse, you will find a brief, prayerful reflection. This is simply what the verse was saying to me, and what I wanted to say to the Lord about it. I encourage you to use this prayer not as a substitute for your own prayer, but rather, a springboard for your own conversation with the Lord.

We sometimes make praying a lot harder than it is. When I first began writing this book, I mentioned that I was working on a mom's prayer book while I was addressing a mother's group. After the talk, a young mom came up to me and said, "I can't wait until your new book comes out. I really want to pray, but I just don't know how to start."

That statement made me sad. I was flattered she was looking forward to my new book, but prayer, to me, is simply talking with God. And talking to a loving parent should never be hard or confusing or too formal. I believe that God is not concerned with how much theology we reflect in our prayers, but rather, how much honesty we reflect. He is not concerned with form and etiquette. He is concerned about us, our hearts and not our heads.

And that's what you will find here: Daily devotions that are actually talks with God, discussions with Jesus and our Blessed

Mother Mary.

This book is designed to be used as a devotional calendar, so you will find special holy days and holidays observed. The difficulty in including some of these days here is that certain special days throughout the year fall on different days each and every year. For example, Easter and Mother's Day float around each year, making them hard to include in a book of devotions that hopes to not be obsolete after one year. But, of course, we cannot have a Mom's devotional calendar without Easter and Mother's Day as well as so many of the other special days. With this in mind, these floating holidays and holy days have been denoted with an asterisk. They may not fall on the right day for the year you are reading it, but I am sure you will figure it out.

After all, you are a mom.

A Catholic Mom.

24/7.

January 1
New Year's Day

But by the grace of God I am what I am, and his grace toward me has not been in vain. On the contrary, I worked harder than any of them—though it was not I, but the grace of God that is with me. 1 Corinthians 15:10

By your grace, dear God, I am a mother. A mother! How can I ever thank you for this amazing grace? How can I ever explain or express the worth of this grace to me? Allow me, Lord, to thank you for the rest of my life, by sharing your grace with others. And help me to never forget that the source of this grace—the root of it all—has nothing to do with me, or how hard I work. But it has everything to do with you.

January 2

She looks well to the ways of her household, and does not eat the bread of idleness. Her children rise up and call her happy; her husband too, and he praises her. Proverbs 31:27-28

I confess, dear Lord, some days I just want a little praise. A little recognition. I want someone to notice the laundry, the house, the food, the kids. Yes, I want praise. But Lord, even if what I do every day seems to be undone by nightfall, help me to remember that my praise may not be in the form of an award or paycheck. Lord, remind me that my praise is found in a child's voice softly whispering, "I love you, Mommy." And for that, I praise you.

JANUARY 3

You prepare a table before me in the presence of my enemies; you anoint my head with oil; my cup overflows. PSALM 23:5

Some days, dear Lord, I feel like my cup does indeed overflow. Help me, though, not to complain all the time about my bountiful blessings. Inspire me to remember that these times pass way too quickly and one day my cup may not be so full. Thank you for these blessings that fill my life so abundantly. And please, Lord Jesus, send me a bigger cup.

JANUARY 4
SAINT ELIZABETH ANN SETON

God will direct it and that is enough. I look neither behind nor before but straight upwards, without thinking of human calculations—it all belongs to God. SAINT ELIZABETH ANN SETON

Dear Lord, help me today to remember these words of this great mother, educator and saint. Help me to finally understand that it is not up to me. It is up to you. And if this day of mothering starts to pull me in so many directions that I begin to feel lost, help me to find my only true direction again by focusing on you, Jesus.

JANUARY 5

As God's chosen ones, holy and beloved, clothe yourselves with compassion, kindness, humility, meekness, and patience. COLOSSIANS 3:12

Sometimes, Lord, I do feel chosen by you. When I consider the extreme honor you have blessed me with to give me the chance to raise my children—your children here on earth—it humbles me. Please help me wear the clothing of compassion, kindness, humility, meekness and patience that I need to fulfill this great vocation you have chosen for me.

JANUARY 6
EPIPHANY*

(*Observed the Sunday after January 1)

On entering the house, they saw the child with Mary his mother; and they knelt down and paid him homage. Then, opening their treasure chests, they offered him gifts of gold, frankincense, and myrrh.
MATTHEW 2:11

Gold. Frankincense. Myrrh. Lord, those are great gifts. But if I had been at the manger, what could I have possibly brought to you? Or for that matter, what can I possibly give to you today? Some days, I have to admit that I feel my gifts are wiping noses and bottoms or drying tears. When I feel unworthy, dear Jesus, please remind me that taking care of your children is worth more than gold, frankincense and myrrh. As a matter of fact, keep reminding me that it is absolutely priceless.

JANUARY 7

Though an army encamp against me, my heart shall not fear; though war rise up against me, yet I will be confident. PSALM 27:3

Dear Lord, I wish I were more confident in my own abilities. When I consider what being a mom really is—how awesome the responsibilities are—I sometimes feel that I am not qualified for this most important job of my life. What if I make a mistake? What if I really mess up? Remind me Lord, that it was your divine wisdom that blessed me with this job. It is all part of your beautiful plan for me. And help me to understand that while I may never be fully confident in myself, I can be eternally confident in you.

JANUARY 8

The Lord is not slow about his promise, as some think of slowness, but is patient with you, not wanting any to perish, but all to come to repentance. 2 PETER 3:9

Patience. O, Lord, how I need patience. Right now! Throughout any given day my patience is put to the test. And, Lord, you know some days I pass the test with flying colors. But before I can even feel my own hand patting myself on my back for this accomplishment, my patience is once again tested. And the next time, I am humbled. I am sorry, Lord, for all the times I have let you down with my lack of patience for my children—your children. Thank you for your merciful love that never lacks patience for me.

JANUARY 9

The sun shall not strike you by day, nor the moon by night. The LORD will keep you from all evil; he will keep your life." PSALM 121:6-7

I never knew what being afraid was before I had children, Lord—not afraid for me—but afraid for them. I want to protect them from all the hurts—physical and emotional—that the world might send their way. Help me translate this powerful parental feeling into a deeper understanding of your love for your children. Gently remind me, Heavenly Father, that as much as I love them, you love them—and all of your children—infinitely more. Grant me peace through that understanding.

January 10

The LORD does not see as mortals see; they look on the outward appearance, but the LORD looks on the heart. 1 SAMUEL 16:7

What do you see, dear Lord, when you look into my heart? Do you see the incredible love I feel for you, for my children, for my entire family? Or is that view clouded by the murkiness of petty jealousies, grudges and wrong thoughts? I am sorry, Jesus, for the ugliness that I sometimes allow to creep into my heart. Please cleanse my heart so that it might be more closely united to your Sacred Heart.

January 11

There are many who say, "O that we might see some good! Let the light of your face shine on us, O LORD!" PSALM 4:6

O, Lord, never in my life have I seen your face shining more clearly on me than each of the precious times when I first looked into the eyes of my newborn babies. Such hope! Such faith! Such love! What a gift you give us, allowing us to hold a tiny bit of heaven in our arms! Thank you, Lord, for the promise of your love you make to us each and every blessed time a baby is born.

JANUARY 12

Listen! I am standing at the door, knocking; if you hear my voice and open the door, I will come in to you and eat with you, and you with me.
REVELATION 3:20

I'm worried, Lord. There are some days when I cannot even hear myself think, let alone hear you knocking at my door. And there are some days when I would be ashamed if you dropped by my home. Prepare me, dear Jesus, for when you do come for me. Please let me be ready—not just my house—but my heart. Please let me hear you. Please knock loudly.

BAPTISM OF JESUS*
(*Sunday after Epiphany)

And when Jesus had been baptized, just as he came up from the water, suddenly the heavens were opened to him and he saw the Spirit of God descending like a dove and alighting on him. And a voice from heaven said, "This is my Son, the Beloved, with whom I am well pleased."
MATTHEW 3:16–17

I want to please you, Lord. I want to think that on any occasion you might open up the heavens and call forth, "This is my beloved daughter, in whom I am well pleased." But I know the truth is, I fall short on so many days. Help me, dear Lord, to live my life in a way that pleases you. And thank you for the gift of eternal life that you gave me, and which you give to each of us at our baptism.

JANUARY 14

The wolf shall live with the lamb, the leopard shall lie down with the kid, the calf and the lion and the fatling together, and a little child shall lead them.
ISAIAH 11:6

Lord, why do we adults insist on labeling everyone? Our children must be so confused.

One day we proudly inform them that everyone is the same. The next, we are adhering invisible labels on everyone who is unique in any given way. Help me, dear Lord, to teach my children to ignore labels and see what is inside a person. Better yet, God, help my children to teach me.

JANUARY 15

Let the words of my mouth and the meditation of my heart be acceptable to you, O LORD, my rock and my redeemer. PSALM 19:14

Today, Lord, please help me to remember that whatever comes out of my mouth falls upon little ears. Whether I think I am spouting witless words or words of wisdom, help me to realize the little people in my life just might be listening. And I know you are always listening, Lord. Grant me the grace of knowing when to bite my tongue.

JANUARY 16

Likewise the Spirit helps us in our weakness; for we do not know how to pray as we ought, but that very Spirit intercedes with sighs too deep for words.
ROMANS 8:26

Dear Lord, so many times I have been able to know that my children need something from me even when they are unable to voice their wants. What a precious connection this is! What a precious gift! Thank you, Lord. And help me today to use that understanding to better comprehend the connection you have with your children. Help me to grasp how much more infinitely wonderful is your ability to know when we need you the most. What a precious gift that is! Help me to trust more and more in that precious gift.

JANUARY 17

Blessed are the peacemakers, for they will be called children of God. MATTHEW 5:9

So many times, Lord, I feel that my main job description is that of peacemaker. It seems I am usually trying to patch up an existing disagreement in my house or avoid a new one altogether. Help me to remember that by doing this, I am being an instrument of your peace, as Saint Francis would say. And help me, Lord, like Saint Francis, to be such an example of peace to my children that they, too, will want to be peacemakers. Until then, dear Lord, help my instrument of your peace to play so loudly that I cannot hear all the bickering.

JANUARY 18

For surely I know the plans I have for you, says the LORD, *plans for your welfare and not for harm, to give you a future with hope.* JEREMIAH 29:11

Lord, you know everything! Why can't I remember that? Why do I try to figure so many things out for myself? Why do I ever doubt that you are in charge and that you already know the plans you have for me? Help me, today, dear God, to let go of more and more of my fears and doubts until I find myself resting in the embrace of the knowledge that you are the most loving parent and you will never leave your child alone.

JANUARY 19

Then when you call upon me and come and pray to me, I will hear you. When you search for me, you will find me; if you seek me with all your heart . . .
JEREMIAH 29:12-13

Lord, I do seek you with all my heart—on most days. But then on some days my heart seems so divided. There is so much to think about, so much to do. I confess that my heart gets easily distracted. It seems like so many people need a piece of my heart. Please help me focus today on you, Lord. Remind me that if I give my heart to everyone else before I first give it to you, in the long run, I have given them nothing.

JANUARY 20
MARTIN LUTHER KING DAY

Everybody can be great because anybody can serve. You don't have to have a college degree to serve. You don't have to make your subject and verb agree to serve. You only need a heart full of grace. A soul generated by love. MARTIN LUTHER KING, JR.

Some days, dear Lord, I have great dreams of how I will serve you. I imagine many people needing me, learning from me and being thankful for me. And I wonder what great place you will send me to so that I can serve you fully like this. And then I realize, Lord, that you are using me in a great way right now. The people who need me, who learn from me and who are thankful for me are the ones in that great place I call my home.

JANUARY 21

See, I am sending you out like sheep into the midst of wolves; so be wise as serpents and innocent as doves. MATTHEW 10:16

Dear Lord, I feel that this is the commission you give to mothers. You need us to be wise as serpents so we can make only the best decisions for your children. You need us to be strong and firm and holy. And yet, you also need us to be kind and soft, and innocent as doves. Gently remind me of these differences. Help me today, dear Jesus, to know when the wise serpent in me needs to dominate and when the innocent dove needs to soar.

JANUARY 22

…for the LORD reproves the one he loves, as a father the son in whom he delights. PROVERBS 3:12

Discipline is hard, Lord. It is so difficult some days to be fair and yet firm, loving and not too lenient. Grant me, please, the grace of knowing how to be a good parent without being overly indulgent. Help me to love my children enough to expect the best from them. Enable me, dear Lord, to discipline out of love and never out of anger.

JANUARY 23

Do not be wise in your own eyes; fear the LORD, and turn away from evil. PROVERBS 3:7

I confess, dear Lord, that some days I think I know it all. My kids all turn to me with their questions and on a really good day I have the answers. But then there are days that humble me. There are days when I can't seem to do anything right. There are days when I don't even know my own phone number. But just as my kids turn to me, please remind me to keep turning to you. That way, right or wrong, I'll at least be going in the right direction.

January 24

Finally, all of you, have unity of spirit, sympathy, love for one another, a tender heart, and a humble mind. 1 PETER 3:8

That's what I want for my family, Lord, unity of spirit, sympathy, love, tender hearts and humble minds. What a perfect world this would be if we all tried for that: first in our families, then in our communities and then in our world. Help us, dear Jesus, to strive for that. Please unite us all. Help us to aim for a little piece of heaven—the peace of heaven— here on earth.

January 25
Conversion of Saint Paul

Rejoice in the Lord always; again I will say, Rejoice. PHILIPPIANS 4:4

Thank you, Lord. Thank you, Lord. Thank you, Lord. So many times, I forget to say that. Thank you! You have blessed my life with wonders I could never have wished for. Yet still, I complain. I ask for more. I forget to say, "thank you." Forgive me, Lord. Help me to make every day of my life a thank-you card for you.

JANUARY 26

Do not worry about anything, but in everything by prayer and supplication with thanksgiving let your requests be made known to God. PHILIPPIANS 4:6

Lord, how many times do I tell my children not to worry? Children have so many fears and anxieties about life, school, the world and each other. But they know they can come to me. They tell me of their fears. We talk about their fears. I listen. I try to reassure them. Sometimes the problem is solved. Sometimes the problem still exists. But the best part is, we talked about it together. Help me, dear Lord, to remember to do the same with you. Remind me always to come to you with my fears. Remind me to talk things over with my loving Father.

JANUARY 27

…but those who wait for the LORD shall renew their strength, they shall mount up with wings like eagles, they shall run and not be weary, they shall walk and not faint. ISAIAH 40:31

Dear God, I confess that I grow weary often. I get tired. My spirit grows weak. Help me to know when this happens that it is because I am trying to get my strength from myself—and I have such a limited supply of it. But you, dear Lord, your strength is abundant. It is never ending. Please remind me that my strength must come from you. It is only with you we can walk, run and eventually fly like the eagles.

JANUARY 28
SAINT THOMAS AQUINAS

The things that we love tell us what we are.
SAINT THOMAS AQUINAS

Sometimes, Lord, we throw around the word "love" too easily. I love that dress. I love that movie. I love chocolate. Today, dear God, help me to truly focus on what I love. Help me to see the preciousness of that word. Help me to see the preciousness of what I deeply love. Thank you for the gifts in my life that are the people around me. Thank you for sending me love in the form of a child.

JANUARY 29

The steadfast love of the LORD never ceases, his mercies never come to an end; they are new every morning; great is your faithfulness.
LAMENTATIONS 3:22-23

Lord, some days I feel all used up. At the end of the day, I feel like I have nothing left to give. Of course, some days I am completely spent by noon. I pray that with your love and your mercy, you will renew *me* every morning. With the dawn of each new day, grant me a new and better supply of patience, faith and love. Lord, please renew me.

JANUARY 30

The LORD is my light and my salvation; whom shall I fear? The LORD is the stronghold of my life; of whom shall I be afraid? PSALM 27:1

Some days, dear Lord, I just want to hold my children close to me and never let them go. It's so scary out there. Sometimes I am so afraid the world will hurt them. I know, precious Jesus, that I can and that I must let go. But I know I can only do this if I truly rest

in the grace that you never let go. Remind me
that we are all held in your loving embrace.

January 31

*See what love the Father has given us, that we
should be called children of God; and that is what
we are.* 1 John 3:1

So many days, Lord, I am focused solely on
being a mom. And I love being a mom. As a
mom, I am calling the shots. I am in charge (at
least I like to pretend I am). But, Lord, I know
that sometimes I need to put aside my "mom
hat" in order to be a submissive child again—
your child. Help me, dear God, to know when
this mom needs to take off her controlling
"mom hat" and put on her listening "child of
God hat." Remind me how wonderful it is to
simply sit with you, my heavenly Father, and
rejoice that you are fully in charge.

FEBRUARY 1

*...as for me and my household, we will serve the
LORD.* JOSHUA 24:15

Forgive me, Lord, that so much of my day is
spent serving the mundane. So often I focus on
the physical things that need to be done.
Laundry, grocery shopping and cleaning may
be necessities in my house, but help me not to
serve them as lord over my house. Truly enable
me to focus more on the spiritual things that
need to be done. Dear Lord, truly enable me
and my home to serve you.

FEBRUARY 2
PRESENTATION OF JESUS

*Whoever becomes humble like this child is the
greatest in the kingdom of heaven.* MATTHEW 18:4

Thank you, dear Lord, for children. They are
so pure and simple. They teach us pure joy.
They explain simple truths. They are one step
closer to you. Today, please help me to start
letting go of the grown-up complications that
keep me from becoming humble as a child.
Help me to learn from my children how to
rejoice in being a child of God.

February 3

…what is impossible for mortals is possible for God.
Luke 18:27

Dear God, sometimes my day seems impossible.
When I look at all the demands on me, I don't
think I can go on. And the truth is—I can't. I
can't do it—but you can. I can't do it. But you
can. Please remind me, Lord, to say that over
and over today, when I feel the weight of the
world is sinking down upon my shoulders. I
can't do it. But you can.

February 4

*Then he went down with them and came to
Nazareth, and was obedient to them. His mother
treasured all these things in her heart.* Luke 2:51

Dear Blessed Mother Mary, how did your heart
hold all that it would have to hold? How did
you do it? Some days I feel that my own heart
will burst with joy. Other days I am certain it
will break with pain. Teach me, dear Mary, to
love as you love. Teach me to be a good
mother. Help me learn to treasure the things in
my heart while I can.

FEBRUARY 5

Come to me, all you that are weary and are
carrying heavy burdens, and I will give you rest.
MATTHEW 11:28

Some days, dear Lord, I find myself dreaming
of a day when I will be able to rest more. A
simple day when I can have an uninterrupted
cup of coffee or maybe even read a book cover
to cover. I sometimes dream of a time when I
will not be needed twenty-four hours a day,
seven days a week. But then, you show me
something that reminds me how quickly this
demanding time passes. You slowly reveal to
me the preciousness of now. Today, when I get
tired, help me to turn to you for strength. Help
me to rest in the knowledge that this time
passes way too quickly. Books and coffee will
always be around. But a childhood lasts but a
moment.

FEBRUARY 6

For this very reason, you must make every effort to
support your faith with goodness, and goodness
with knowledge, and knowledge with self-control,
and self-control with endurance, and endurance
with godliness, and godliness with mutual affection,
and mutual affection with love. 2 PETER 1:5–7

Lord, some days I feel lucky if I have had a chance to take a shower. How can I possibly find time for all the matters of faith that I neglect? How can I possibly focus on goodness and knowledge and godliness and endurance when I am focused on runny noses, dirty clothes and fussy babies? Today, Lord, help me to find you in all the busy-ness of my day.

FEBRUARY 7

...but he said to me, "My grace is sufficient for you, for power is made perfect in weakness." So, I will boast all the more gladly of my weaknesses, so that the power of Christ may dwell in me.
2 CORINTHIANS 12:9

Dear God, if we are supposed to boast in our weaknesses, I have a lot to boast about. Remind me when I am feeling unworthy and low that you are there ready to turn an ungodly moment into a Godly moment. Help me to remember that sometimes I have to get to the bottom before you can take me to the top.

FEBRUARY 8

You open your hand, satisfying the desire of every living thing. PSALM 145:16

How incredible your hand is, Lord! I can see your hand in the glorious setting of the sun and the mighty roar of the ocean. But those are the big things. I think I marvel most when I see your hand in the smaller things, Lord. I see your hand in chocolate-covered lips that sweetly kiss my cheek. I see your hand in the soft sigh of a baby as it sleeps on my chest. Thank you, Jesus, for giving me a hand whenever I need it the most.

FEBRUARY 9

I am the vine, you are the branches. Those who abide in me and I in them bear much fruit, because apart from me you can do nothing. JOHN 15:5

Lord, I want to grow in faith with you today. But my day is already so busy. When will I find time to read the Bible or pray? Help me, dear God, to understand that my faith is like a fragile flower. If I don't take care of it and water it and nurture it, it will eventually wither and die. Remind me to daily water my faith

with your living water and to nurture it with
your life-giving Word.

FEBRUARY 10
SAINT SCHOLASTICA

*Whatever you ask for in prayer with faith, you will
receive.* MATTHEW 21:22

Dear God, all the great saints knew the power
of prayer. I know the power of prayer, too. But
sometimes I forget to use the precious power
that has been given to us, a power we have
done absolutely nothing to deserve. It is a gift:
a beautiful and priceless gift. But so many
times, it becomes a gift we know the value of,
but forget to use. Lord, teach me to pray. Help
me to talk to you. Help me to listen.

FEBRUARY 11

As for mortals, their days are like grass; they flourish like a flower of the field; for the wind passes over it, and it is gone, and its place knows it no more. PSALM 103:15-16

It's all going so quickly, Lord. There was a time when I felt that one particular stage would never end. I suspected I would be changing diapers and wearing spit-up forever. But, Lord it goes so quickly. So very quickly. Remind me of those fleeting yesterdays to keep me from wishing away the preciousness of today.

FEBRUARY 12
LINCOLN'S BIRTHDAY

Cast all your anxiety on him, because he cares for you. 1 PETER 5:7

Dear Lord, I don't think my children will ever come close to understanding the depth of my love for them—until, perhaps, they have children of their own. And yet as deep as this love is, as passionate as I feel it, I know that it cannot begin to compare to your unending love for us. And while I may not be able to comprehend such greatness of love, it still comforts me, Lord. It comforts me, it thrills me, it moves me—just knowing there exists such a great love for me.

FEBRUARY 13

Light dawns for the righteous, and joy for the upright in heart. PSALM 97:11

Lord, sometimes the world seems so dark. The nightly news reports of war and terrorism and violence close to home. It would be easy to assume that the evil and sin of the world was winning. But you, Lord, are the light of the world. You bring us joy. You have already claimed a victory over sin and death. Shine on me today so that I might shine for others. Please shine on me.

FEBRUARY 14
SAINT VALENTINE'S DAY

I give you a new commandment, that you love one another. Just as I have loved you, you also should love one another. JOHN 13:34

Lord, it is easy for me to feel love for my children with my every breath. It is natural for me to see you in them. But, I feel I fall short in loving you through my husband and others. I do love them Lord, but I get so caught up in the mommy role that I sometimes forget about my other roles in life. Please, dear Jesus, gently remind me to tell all those that I love dearly that I do love them. And help me to do this with actions as well as words.

FEBRUARY 15

Make a joyful noise to the LORD, all the earth. PSALM 100:1

Lord, you know the sounds in my house are sometimes less than joyful. Sometimes there is bickering and short tempers bouncing around the rooms. And that is just the adults in the house. Help me, Lord, to set a good example

for my household. Help me to make more
joyful noises than unpleasant ones. And please,
Lord, let the joyful noises echo back to me.

FEBRUARY 16

*We know that all things work together for good for
those who love God...* ROMANS 8:28

Dear God, sometimes I just can't see it.
Sometimes I am looking for the reason
something bad has happened—the
explanation—and I just don't see it. Sometimes
I try to see where your hand is in something
that appears to be void of any good—and I
can't find it. Please help me in these times to
remember that everything will work out
because you are never far away. Remind me,
dear Lord, that you are with me always. And
please, help me to see you even when—
especially when—my eyes are clenched tightly
in fear.

FEBRUARY 17

*And my God will fully satisfy every need of yours
according to his riches in glory in Christ Jesus.*
PHILIPPIANS 4:19

Sometimes, Lord, my children will passionately
beg for something they feel they absolutely
must have. And I smile and understand that it
is not at all what they need. I don't give in
because I know better than they do what they
need. Sometimes this leads to a temper
tantrum, but eventually it works out for the
best. Please remind me of this insight the next
time I am passionately begging you for
something that I am sure that I absolutely
need. Remind me that you know infinitely
better than I do what is best for me. And
please, Lord, help me not to throw a temper
tantrum when I don't get what I want.

FEBRUARY 18
*PRESIDENT'S DAY

(Observed 3rd Monday of February)

*Keep your lives free from the love of money, and be
content with what you have; for he has said, "I will
never leave you or forsake you." HEBREWS 13:5*

It is hard not to get caught up in the love of money, Lord. It seems like everything in the world comes with a price tag on it. We love money. We love the power we feel it brings us when we buy things. Guide us to overlook the trappings of a commercial world and keep our focus solely on you. Help us to get over that love of the power of money. Enable us instead to embrace the power of your love.

FEBRUARY 19

For God so loved the world that he gave his only Son, so that everyone who believes in him may not perish but may have eternal life. JOHN 3:16

You gave us your son, God. Your son, your only child. Knowing what was to happen— knowing the pain and the suffering—you gave your child to the world so that we would believe. How it must break your heart when we still falter, when we still doubt and when we still sin. You gave so much. And yet some days, we give you so little. Please forgive us, Lord. Forgive us our ingratitude.

*But when he noticed the strong wind, he became
frightened, and beginning to sink, he cried out,
"Lord, save me!" Jesus immediately reached out his
hand and caught him, saying to him, "You of little
faith, why did you doubt?"* MATTHEW 14:30-31

Some days, Lord, it is easy to walk strongly in
faith. All is going well and I feel like I have it
all figured out. But then life begins to
happen—things start to go wrong. And as the
waves of worry and fear smack me in my face,
I too, feel like I am sinking. When this
happens, please remind me to call out to you,
dear Jesus. For I know you will be there to
take my hand and help me through the storms
of life. But I have to remember to call out to
you. I have to stop doubting.

*Trust in the LORD with all your heart, and do not
rely on your own insight.* PROVERBS 3:5

I confess, Lord, that I have gotten a little too
sure of myself. I rely on my own insight too
much. But, I'm a mom. I have to have great
instincts and insights. I have to stay one step
ahead of everyone. Don't I? But I guess if I am

one step ahead of you, I am one step away from where I really should be. Help me Lord, to find the blend of being self-confident without being self-governing. Help me to stay in step with you. Remind me to let you lead.

FEBRUARY 22
WASHINGTON'S BIRTHDAY

If we confess our sins, he who is faithful and just will forgive us our sins and cleanse us from all unrighteousness. 1 JOHN 1:9

Why is it so hard for a child to say, "I'm sorry?" Some days my children opt for sitting in *time-out* for several minutes, instead of muttering a simple apology that would only take two seconds. Why is it so hard for them to say: "I admit this. I did this. I'm sorry?" But, Lord, I guess that must be what you are wondering about all of your children. Why is it so hard for us to confess our sins? Why is it hard for us to say: "I admit this. I did this. I'm sorry." Help me today to confess my sins. And if I forget, I will try to understand when I get a *time-out* along the way.

FEBRUARY 23

When they call to me, I will answer them; I will be with them in trouble, I will rescue them and honor them. PSALM 91:15

It is so simple, dear Jesus. It is so simple and yet we make it so complicated. You are there for us. You are always there for us. All we have to do is call on you. Why do we insist on making it harder? Why do we try to do it on our own? Forgive us for being such stubborn children. And thank you for being such a patient parent.

FEBRUARY 24

...do not provoke your children to anger, but bring them up in the discipline and instruction of the Lord. EPHESIANS 6:4

How am I doing today, Lord? Am I finding that blend of firm discipline mixed with merciful love? Am I doing okay in not losing my temper and yet not letting my children get away with the actions I know need to be corrected? I think I am doing fine so far, dear Lord. But any minute now the kids will actually wake up. Help me as this day begins.

FEBRUARY 25

In all your ways acknowledge him, and he will make straight your paths. PROVERBS 3:6

Some days, Lord, my path doesn't seem straight at all. In fact, some days, I don't even think I have a path. I seem to be going nowhere—fast. I feel caught up on a treadmill of life—going through the motions and yet accomplishing so little. Remind me Lord, that I am going somewhere every day when I wake up. Help me walk in the right direction. And keep me on the path you have chosen for me. But first, please help me find it.

FEBRUARY 26

I can do all things through him who strengthens me. PHILIPPIANS 4:13

Everyday, Lord, I can see an advertisement for something that promises to make me thinner, stronger, more beautiful. There are million-dollar industries thriving because we all want to be better than we are. Remind me, dear Lord that everything I want to be and do, can come true, if I do it through you. And what is more, this gift is free because you have already paid the price for us all.

...for we walk by faith, not by sight. 2 CORINTHIANS 5:7

We moms are pretty good about walking by
faith and not by sight, aren't we, Lord? You
know we don't do what we do for the pay. We
don't do what we do for the recognition. We
don't do what we do because we see the results
everyday. No, we do what we do because we
believe it is important. We understand it is
good. We have faith that it is the most
important job you have given us. Help me
today, Lord, to walk in faith even when the
rest of the world beckons me to come and
walk by sight.

For truly I tell you, if you have faith the size of a mustard seed, you will say to this mountain, "Move from here to there," and it will move; and nothing will be impossible for you.
MATTHEW 17:20

Lord, I confess I never understood the story of the mustard seed before. I mean, how could faith that small move mountains? How could anything that small be worth that much? Then I held a newborn baby in my arms. And I understood. Faith, even in the smallest packages, is precious. It is a gift. Thank you, Lord for the gift of faith. Remind me to open it everyday.

MARCH 1
ASH WEDNESDAY*

Jesus said to him, "I am the way, and the truth, and the life. No one comes to the Father except through me." JOHN 14:6

You came for me, Lord. You came for me! Nothing I could possibly do could ever make me worthy of your loving me that much, but still you do. You love me enough to live and die for me and for us all. Help me today to try to grasp the magnitude of that fact. Help me today to truly make you my way, my truth and my life.

MARCH 2

No one has ever seen God; if we love one another, God lives in us, and his love is perfected in us. 1 JOHN 4:12

Lord, nowhere is it easier for me to see your perfect love than when I look at a newborn baby, who is so precious and perfect. It is easy to see you in such perfection. It is easy to love you in this perfection. How is it then, dear God, that I so quickly forget to look for you in the grown-ups that I meet every day? Today,

please help me to seek you in all that I meet.
Help me to find you everywhere I go.

MARCH 3
SAINT KATHERINE DREXEL

Peacefully do at each moment what at that moment needs to be done. SAINT KATHERINE DREXEL

Today, dear God, I ask you to help me find some of the willing and generous spirit that beautifully radiated from Saint Katherine Drexel. Help me to give without asking the cost to myself. Help me to think of others before myself. Help me to become less selfish and more selfless. Help me to humbly do at each moment what at each moment needs to be done. And if I manage to do this, please keep my hands folded in prayer so that it becomes impossible to pat myself on the back.

MARCH 4

Above all, maintain constant love for one another, for love covers a multitude of sins. 1 PETER 4:8

It's all about love, isn't it, Lord? I have come to discover this verse to be so true. Love does cover a multitude of sins. Any mother knows this. We can forgive our kids most anything due to the love we feel for them. And yet, why do we still doubt that you can forgive us our sins? Why do we not understand that because you love better, deeper, more perfectly than we love, so too do you forgive better, deeper, more perfectly? Help us to learn this today, tomorrow and the day after...

MARCH 5

As a mother comforts her child, so I will comfort you. ISAIAH 66:13

Today, dear God, as I hold one of my children in my arms to comfort them for one reason or another, remind me that your arms are constantly wrapped around me. Every time I kiss a boo-boo, every time I wipe a tear, let me feel you beside me doing the same. Enable me, precious Jesus, to feel your loving embrace as I go through my day.

MARCH 6

Little children, let us love, not in word or speech, but in truth and action. 1 JOHN 3:18

Lord, what do my actions say? It is one thing for me to monitor the things my kids hear me say. But what are they hearing when I am quiet? What are they learning from me when I ignore a poor man on the street? What do they hear when I pretend not to be home in order to avoid talking on the phone to someone? Today, Lord, please help me to teach love not just in words, but in actions as well.

MARCH 7

Every generous act of giving, with every perfect gift, is from above, coming down from the Father of lights, with whom there is no variation or shadow due to change. JAMES 1:17

You never change, do you, dear Lord? You never change. So many days, I feel I am surrounded by change. My children change from being babies and toddlers one day to becoming teenagers and adults almost overnight. And I'm changing, Lord. Wasn't I just a young girl not too long ago? And now I am a mother with my own children. So many changes. It is more than reassuring to know that through it all, you never change.

MARCH 8

In return—I speak as to children—open wide your hearts also. 2 CORINTHIANS 6:13

Lord, you know that no one opens his heart as wide as a child. Children want to be friends with everyone they meet. They want to dance and play the day away. They want to love with all their hearts. But somehow we adults teach them unspoken lessons about closing their hearts—not trusting everyone. We teach them fear. Today, dear Lord, let me learn from my children how to open wide my heart. Help me to love with all my heart once again.

MARCH 9

Let all that you do be done in love. 1 CORINTHIANS 16:14

Some days, Lord, I worry so much. I worry that I am not doing it right. What if I really mess this motherhood thing up? It is so important. There are so many things I can do wrong. Please help me to remember that everything I do—if I do it in love—with love—based in love, it may not always work out the way I had planned, but somehow it will work out.

MARCH 10

O LORD, I have heard of your renown, and I stand in awe, O LORD, of your work. HABAKKUK 3:2

I do stand in awe of your work, God. How awesome you are! The oceans, the mountains, the deserts make me gasp. The rising and the setting of the sun make me cry. And babies. And children. All uniquely different. All uniquely perfect. Well done, God! Well done.

MARCH 11

We love because he first loved us. 1 JOHN 4:19

What an amazing thing love is, Lord. It can
make us laugh. It can make us cry. It has the
power to make the young feel old and the old
feel young. What a pure and wonderful gift it
is to love someone. What a pure and
wonderful gift it is to be loved by someone.
And it began with you. Thank you, Lord, for
loving us first.

MARCH 12

*Do your best to present yourself to God as one
approved by him, a worker who has no need to be
ashamed, rightly explaining the word of truth.*
2 TIMOTHY 2:15

How will I present myself to you today, dear
Lord? Will it be as a worker who has no need
to be ashamed? Or will it be as a sinner
covered in shame? Will I be explaining the
word of truth today? Or will my tongue
become so twisted it will be a wonder I can
even speak? Guide me today, Dear Lord. Help
me to be as one who is approved by you.

Love is patient; love is kind; love is not envious or boastful or arrogant or rude. It does not insist on its own way; it is not irritable or resentful.
1 CORINTHIANS 13:4-5

Lord, you know I love my family dearly. And yet you know that many times I am not as patient with them as I should be. You know I adore my children. And yet some times my thoughts and words may be less than kind. Guide me today to strive to be more loving. Help me to love better. Help me to love as you love.

MARCH 14

[Love] does not rejoice in wrongdoing, but rejoices in the truth. It bears all things, believes all things, hopes all things, endures all things. 1 CORINTHIANS 13:6-7

Dear God, some days we forget we are all in this together. We are on the same team. So many days, I have to remind my children of that fact. And maybe some days they need to remind me. We are on the same team. When one of us is hurting, we all are hurting. Remind us all that the world might knock us down, but a family picks us up. And it is your love, dear Lord, that holds us together.

MARCH 15

But you are a God ready to forgive, gracious and merciful, slow to anger and abounding in steadfast love, and you did not forsake them. NEHEMIAH 9:17

Lord, you are the perfect parent. Some days I feel I am a parent who is ready to forgive, gracious and merciful, slow to anger and abounding in steadfast love. Those are good days. But too many days, I am not any of those wonderful things. Too often, I feel quick to judge, temperamental and abounding in qualities that have little to do with love. Help me today to be a better parent than I was yesterday.

MARCH 16

Your steadfast love, O LORD, extends to the heavens, your faithfulness to the clouds. PSALM 36:5

When one of my children was in preschool he would say, "I love you from here to heaven and back again." That was his way, Lord, of trying to put into words his grasp of the love he was feeling. Guide me to use that idea, multiplying it infinitely over and over and over, to get an idea of the love you have for us. Thank you, Lord. You truly love us from here to heaven and back again.

MARCH 17
SAINT PATRICK

This day I call to me, God's strength to direct me, God's power to sustain me, God's wisdom to guide me. SAINT PATRICK

How wise Saint Patrick was, dear Lord! How wise he was to ask for your strength, power and wisdom to help him through his day. He knew he couldn't do all you had called him to do simply by his own strength, power and wisdom. Why do I try to get by on my own merits so often? Why do I set myself up to fail? Today Lord, I too, ask for your strength to direct me, your power to sustain me, and your wisdom to guide me.

MARCH 18

... let me fall into the hand of the LORD, for his mercy is very great. 1 CHRONICLES 21:13

Some days, Lord, I do feel I am falling. I feel I am falling out of control of everything. But then again, I guess that is what you are trying to tell me, isn't it? I need to lose control—I need to give up control. I need to realize that you are in control...not me. Today, dear Lord,

help me to lose control…to you. Help me to
fall into your hands.

MARCH 19
SAINT JOSEPH

*When Joseph awoke from sleep, he did as the angel
of the Lord commanded him; he took her as his
wife…* MATTHEW 1:24

Dear Saint Joseph, you showed such silent
strength. You were there when you needed to
be. You allowed yourself to be used by God
even though you must have had so many
questions! Please help me today to find such
silent strength—such trust. Help me to listen
to the Lord even when I don't understand
completely—even when I have so many
questions.

MARCH 20

Although you have not seen him, you love him; and even though you do not see him now, you believe in him and rejoice with an indescribable and glorious joy. 1 PETER 1:8

Lord, there is a beautiful faith that comes with pregnancy or awaiting the arrival of a new child. We have not yet met our new family member—and yet we love him. We cannot see him, yet we believe and rejoice with such joy awaiting his arrival. This must be what you are telling us about our faith. Although we cannot see you, we can love you. We believe in you. We rejoice in waiting to meet you, Lord. This is faith. This is love.

MARCH 21
SPRING EQUINOX/SAINT BENEDICT

Listen carefully to the Master's instructions, and attend to them with the ear of your heart.
RULE OF SAINT BENEDICT

Dear God, help me to listen in prayer like the insightful monk, Saint Benedict. Help me to understand that prayer is meant to be a dialogue, not just a monologue. I confess that too many days find me with just enough time for my side of the conversation. I don't spend enough time listening for you to respond. Help me today, dear Lord, to take the necessary time I need to fully listen with the ear of my heart.

March 22

Hide your face from my sins, and blot out all my iniquities. Psalm 51:9

Oh, Lord, how I wish you could hide your face from my sins! But I know you see it all. You see every impurity—every thought and action that is so much less than my best. Please help me today, dear Lord, to see what it is I need to change the most. Help me to stop hiding my face from my own sins.

MARCH 23

Two are better than one, because they have a good reward for their toil. For if they fall, one will lift up the other; but woe to one who is alone and falls and does not have another to help. ECCLESIASTES 4:9-10

We need each other, Lord. You have told us this over and over. We need each other. We need you. And yet so many times, we try to do things on our own. Why do we make things harder than they are? Help us to reach out our hands to each other. Dear Lord, help us to reach out our hands to you.

MARCH 24

The LORD will fight for you, and you have only to keep still. EXODUS 14:14

Keep still. Lord, it is very hard for me to keep still. I am too busy. Too busy checking things off my list of things to do. There are things to clean, things to buy, things to do. And when I finally do sit down with my list completed, I am usually thinking of what to put on my next list. Help me Lord, to keep still so that I will feel you more in my life. Please remind me to put you at the top of my list.

March 25
Annunciation of Jesus

Then Mary said, "Here am I, the servant of the Lord; let it be with me according to your word." Then the angel departed from her. Luke 1:38

Weren't you afraid, Mary? You were so young, so innocent . . . and yet so trusting. But without a second thought, you accepted the unbelievable message given to you. I don't think I could have said yes, just like that. I would have asked for a second opinion. I would have suggested another way. Dear Mother Mary, help me today to be more accepting. Help me to open my arms and heart to embrace the Lord's plan for me, instead of pushing it away. Help me to be a better servant of the Lord.

MARCH 26

How very good and pleasant it is when kindred live together in unity! PSALM 133:1

Unity. Oh, Lord, some days that is a foreign word in my house. Some days it seems everyone in this house is going his or her own direction with his or her own interest at heart. Help us today, dear Lord, to find unity. Please help us today to be one with each other and one with you.

MARCH 27

If you, O LORD, should mark iniquities, LORD, who could stand? But there is forgiveness with you, so that you may be revered. PSALM 130:3-4

Dear God, some days, I assume it is my job to mark everyone's iniquities. I appoint myself judge and jury of what everyone else is doing wrong. Help me to try to grasp the idea that you and you alone are the perfect one. And please remind me that you and you alone are the judge of us. My heavenly Father, please help me to love people more, and judge them less.

MARCH 28

I wait for the LORD, my soul waits, and in his word I hope. PSALM 130:5

Waiting is so hard for children, Lord. Today is always better than tomorrow. Now is far superior to later. Yes, children have a hard time with waiting. And, of course, we are all your children. We all need help in learning to wait with hope instead of fear and anxiousness. Today, dear Lord, fill my soul with peaceful hope as I wait for you to answer me.

MARCH 29

Create in me a clean heart, O God, and put a new and right spirit within me. PSALM 51:10

So many times, dear Lord, I am concerned with cleaning other people's hearts and minds. It is too easy to see where others are falling short. But it is so hard to turn this judgmental light I shine on others unto myself. Please dear Lord, help me to remember that when one finger is pointing at someone else, there are three pointing back at me. Show me what I need to change today. Create in me a clean heart, O God.

MARCH 30

O my strength, I will sing praises to you, for you, O God, are my fortress, the God who shows me steadfast love. PSALM 59:17

Some days, dear Lord, I am so concerned with finding someone to sing my praises that I completely forget to sing praises to the one who truly deserves it. Some days I am thirsting for a little praise and recognition. Some days I just want someone to notice their clean clothes, hot food and perhaps comment on these tasks that don't get done on their own. Help me, though, dear Lord to focus on praising you instead of waiting for praise from my family. Heaven knows when that praise might come.

MARCH 31

So let us not grow weary in doing what is right, for we will reap at harvest time, if we do not give up.
GALATIANS 6:9

Some days it would seem easy to give up, Lord. I watch the nightly news. I read the papers. It can be so sad. Sometimes, I wonder how a simple mom can make a difference in a world that seems so wrong. It's enough to make me want to give up. But then I see the children of the world, Lord. I see the hope, the love and the trust in their eyes. And I see faith in a future. Help me today, not to grow weary in doing what is right.

APRIL 1
APRIL FOOL'S DAY

The clever do all things intelligently, but the fool displays folly. PROVERBS 13:16

Lord, I used to feel intelligent. I used to feel like I knew so much. But lately, my reasoning seems ridiculous, and my logic appears laughable. I have even begun to answer all questions with the mother of all explanations, "Because I said so!" Today, dear Lord, help me think before I speak. If I must be a fool today, please help me to be a quiet one.

APRIL 2

Honor everyone. Love the family of believers. 1 PETER 2:17

Lord, I want us to be a family of believers. But what am I teaching my family to believe in today? Am I teaching them to believe in sports and movie stars? Am I teaching them to exalt the rich and famous? Help me, dear Lord, to raise a family of believers who honor everyone—but believe only in you.

APRIL 3

See if there is any wicked way in me, and lead me in the way everlasting. PSALM 139:24

Dear God, some days I see my need for improvement glaring at me from every corner of my life. I know my need for you then, more than ever. But I confess, Lord, that some days, I think I am doing okay, walking the right path and that I am on the right track. I know that these are the most dangerous times for me. Help me on those days to not get caught up in myself, but to always allow myself to get caught up in you.

APRIL 4

… hope does not disappoint us, because God's love has been poured into our hearts through the Holy Spirit that has been given to us. ROMANS 5:5

How generous your gifts of the Holy Spirit are, dear Lord! How amazing! Help me today to empty my heart of all that is not you so that you can fill it with all the graces you want me to have. Fill me, Lord! Pour your love into my heart.

April 5

But my eyes are turned toward you, O God, my
LORD; in you I seek refuge; do not leave me
defenseless. PSALM 141:8

So many days, Lord, my children will turn to
me with their hands outstretched and they will
ask for my help. They want me to protect
them. They want me to help and hold them
close. Remind me today, dear Lord, that this is
what you want me to do when I am troubled.
Today, when I need help, remind me to turn
my hands and my heart to you. Thank you for
patiently waiting there to protect, help and
hold me.

April 6

For this reason a man will leave his father and
mother and be joined to his wife, and the two will
become one flesh. EPHESIANS 5:31

Becoming one flesh is hard, Lord. What's more,
it sounds painful. And sometimes it is painful.
It's hard not to think and act as two. Help my
husband and me today and every day to strive
to be one flesh. Remind us that we are in this
together. Help us to take care of each other, as
we each want to be taken care of.

APRIL 7

Be very careful, therefore, to love the LORD your God. JOSHUA 23:11

We need to be careful with love, don't we Lord? We tend to throw it around like it is not important at all. We take it for granted. We abuse it. Help me, today, to give love the tender treatment it deserves. Enable me today, dear Lord, to give people the tender love they deserve.

APRIL 8

Do not be conformed to this world, but be transformed by the renewing of your minds, so that you may discern what is the will of God—what is good and acceptable and perfect. ROMANS 12:2

Lord, it is so easy to be concerned with conforming to this world. Everyday we see on TV and in magazines what we have to do to make the world love us. Do we need to lose weight? Do we need to make more money? Or do we just need to buy better clothes? Remove from me, Lord, all the world's desires for me. Fill me instead with your desires for me. Fill me with your will.

APRIL 9

My child, if your heart is wise, my heart too will be glad. PROVERBS 23:15

My dear God, over the years, I have brought to you my broken heart, my angry heart, my sad heart and my confused heart. And each time I have asked you to heal the deep wounds of my heart. And each of those precious times you did. But today, dear God, let me bring to you a wise heart, a heart that has you at the center and is, therefore, not only wise, but also glad. Help me, dear Lord, to be wise.

APRIL 10
PALM SUNDAY*

So they took branches of palm trees and went out to meet him, shouting, "Hosanna! Blessed is the one who comes in the name of the Lord—the King of Israel!" JOHN 12:13

What would I have done, dear Lord, if I had been there 2000 years ago? Would I have met you in the street with palm branches? Would I have sung your praises? Or would I have been too busy to attend? This week, dear Jesus, let me be there. Let me meet you wherever I go.

APRIL 11
MONDAY OF HOLY WEEK*

Very truly, I tell you, unless a grain of wheat falls into the earth and dies, it remains just a single grain; but if it dies, it bears much fruit. JOHN 12: 24

You knew you were sent here to die for us. You knew all along. And yet you joyfully came and you patiently taught and you loved us all. It is so hard for us to understand this sacrifice, dear Lord, because we are so weak of heart. Forgive us this weakness. Please help us to find our strength in you.

APRIL 12
TUESDAY OF HOLY WEEK*

And going a little farther, he threw himself on the ground and prayed, "My Father, if it is possible, let this cup pass from me; yet not what I want but what you want." MATTHEW 26:39

So many times, dear Jesus, I too have asked God to take away a cup of suffering. I have begged. I have pleaded. But I was not so wise as to understand that it is always his will, not my own, that needs to be done. The next time I must drink from the cup of suffering, and we all know there will be a next time, help me to find the grace that you showed in the garden of Gethsemane. Help me drink from the cup I am given. Please help me.

APRIL 13
WEDNESDAY OF HOLY WEEK*

But Jesus turned to them and said, "Daughters of Jerusalem, do not weep for me, but weep for yourselves and for your children." LUKE 23:28

I do want to weep for you Lord. Every time I hear of your Passion and your death, I want to weep like I am hearing it for the first time. And, yes, I know the great ending, which is the resurrection, means a great beginning for us all. Still I weep for you, dear Lord. I weep for your pain, your agony, the excruciating suffering that you endured, and yes, I weep for us, your children.

APRIL 14
HOLY THURSDAY*

After he had washed their feet, had put on his robe, and had returned to the table, he said to them, "Do you know what I have done to you?" JOHN 13:12

We mothers are good at serving, Lord. It is what we do. It's part of the job description. And yes, you asked us on that special night to serve each other as you have served us. But, Lord, I confess, I do not always serve the way you served. You served us willingly, lovingly and with a happy heart. Oh, Lord, help me to do that! Today, help me to serve better. Please enable me to truly understand what you were teaching that precious night.

APRIL 15
GOOD FRIDAY*

Then Jesus, crying with a loud voice, said, "Father, into your hands I commend my spirit." Having said this, he breathed his last. LUKE 23:46

You died for me, dear Jesus. You died for my family. You died for us. My dear Lord, you died for us.

APRIL 16
HOLY SATURDAY*

Then Joseph bought a linen cloth, and taking down the body, wrapped it in the linen cloth, and laid it in a tomb that had been hewn out of the rock. He then rolled a stone against the door of the tomb. MARK 15:46

Dear Mother Mary, how did you do it? How your heart must have shattered! How you must have cried! You had to watch your beloved son—your only child—endure a hideously cruel death. When the cruelty was over, did you get to hold him in your arms one last time? Did you try to wipe the blood from his wounded body? How did you do it, Blessed Mother Mary? How did you do it?

April 17
Easter Sunday*

They put him to death by hanging him on a tree; but God raised him on the third day and allowed him to appear. Acts 10:39-40

How can I ever thank you, Lord for enduring Good Friday for me? How can I ever thank you for the gift of Easter Sunday—your resurrection and all the hope, promise and love that came with it? Let me start today. Thank you, Lord. Thank you, Lord. Thank you, Lord.

April 18

Blessed be the God and Father of our Lord Jesus Christ! By his great mercy he has given us a new birth into a living hope through the resurrection of Jesus Christ from the dead. 1 Peter 1:3

How kind and merciful you are, dear God! You have given us the gift of your son, Jesus Christ. You have given us the gift of everlasting life. We will never be able to out-give you, God. We will never be able to pay back this debt. Please, though, allow us to live our lives trying to pay you back. Allow us all to die trying.

APRIL 19

Rid yourselves, therefore, of all malice, and all guile, insincerity, envy, and all slander. Like newborn infants, long for the pure, spiritual milk, so that by it you may grow into salvation. 1 PETER 2:1-2

Why do we hunger, Lord, for that which is wrong for us? Why is the forbidden fruit so often the most tempting fruit of all? Today, dear Lord, help me to turn away from malice, insincerity and envy. Instead, instill in me a thirst for your pure, spiritual milk. Please quench my thirst with your salvation.

APRIL 20

He himself bore our sins in his body on the cross, so that, free from sins, we might live for righteousness; by his wounds you have been healed. 1 PETER 2:24

How much pain your wounds must have caused you, Lord Jesus! And every time we turn away from you in sin, we must cause your wounds to be ripped open again. How much pain we cause you when we sin! Please forgive us, dear Lord. Help us to live for righteousness. Help us to live deserving such incredible forgiveness.

APRIL 21

When he was at the table with them, he took bread, blessed and broke it, and gave it to them. Then their eyes were opened, and they recognized him; and he vanished from their sight. LUKE 24:30-31

If you walked into my house, Lord, would I recognize you? Would my eyes be opened to see that it was indeed you? How many times, Lord, do I not see you dwelling in my house? How many times have I not recognized you in my very own home? Today, open my eyes to you, Lord. Please open my eyes.

April 22

*You did not choose me but I chose you. And I
appointed you to go and bear fruit, fruit that will
last, so that the Father will give you whatever you
ask him in my name.* JOHN 15:16

Thank you for choosing me, dear Lord.
Thank you for choosing me! Please help this
appointment you have given me to bear fruit.
Please guide my life today so that the fruit that
yields from it will be sweet and productive and
not bitter and useless.

April 23

*On the glorious splendor of your majesty, and on
your wondrous works, I will meditate.* PSALM 145:5

Thank you, dear God. Thank you! Your works
are indeed wonderful. Help me to meditate on
this wonder. Help me to think of your glorious
splendor the next time I get worried or
anxious or fearful. My problems may not
immediately disappear. But I'm sure to be in a
better mood while I'm waiting.

April 24

Desire without knowledge is not good, and one who moves too hurriedly misses the way. PROVERBS 19:2

Dear God, you know that the world is made up of so many desires. We think we know what we desire. We think we know what would make us happy. But you know the truth, God. You are the truth. Help me today to pass up on my worldly desires. Enable me, please, to embrace what you desire for me.

April 25

Buy truth, and do not sell it; buy wisdom, instruction, and understanding. PROVERBS 23:23

We think we can buy everything today, don't we, Lord? We think everything is for sale. Everything has a price tag. Help me to understand today that the most precious gift of your truth that you bring to the world is free. Help me not to sell this truth, but to give it away freely to everyone I meet.

APRIL 26

I have said this to you, so that in me you may have peace. In the world you face persecution. But take courage; I have conquered the world! JOHN 16:33

Why do we think that we have to conquer the world, Lord? Why do we think we have to raise our children to conquer the world? It is such a scary idea. The world is such a scary place. Help me today to see that this worry—this anxiety—this fear is all so pointless. You have already conquered the world for us all. You have offered us peace. Help us today to accept your gift of peace.

APRIL 27

And may the Lord make you increase and abound in love for one another and for all, just as we abound in love for you. 1 THESSALONIANS 3:12

Today dear Lord, help the people in my home to increase and abound in love for each other. Even if tempers begin to flare, feelings get stepped on and we all show how imperfect we really are, please help the love never to dwindle. Enable our love for each other to grow and grow in spite of our weaknesses.

He said to him the third time, "Simon son of John, do you love me?" Peter felt hurt because he said to him the third time, "Do you love me?" And he said to him, "Lord, you know everything; you know that I love you." Jesus said to him, "Feed my sheep."
JOHN 21:17

Lord, when one of my children asks me for food, is that you asking me if I love you? When someone in my home needs clean clothes, help with homework, someone to listen to him or her, is that you asking me if I love you? Help me to hear those words of your gentle voice reminding me that I am loving you when I am loving them. Remind me of that incredible fact even when the voices making the requests are not so gentle.

APRIL 29
SAINT CATHERINE OF SIENA

Treat your possessions as if they were on loan from God. SAINT CATHERINE OF SIENA

How wise this saint was, Lord! No wonder popes and kings all listened to her advice. For all of our possessions are, indeed, on loan to us from you. And yet we forget this. We pretend everything we have is ours: our homes, our careers, even our children. We think they will last forever. Forgive us for this ignorance. Gently remind us that all belongs to you. Thank you for the incredible gifts you have loaned to me today!

APRIL 30

And let us consider how to provoke one another to love and good deeds. HEBREWS 10:24

Lord, you know there is a lot of provoking going on at my house, but I am afraid to say it is not provoking one another to love and good deeds. Why does it seem to be so much easier, and more fun, to bring out each other's faults instead of each other's good qualities? Help us today to lovingly encourage each other along our way. Help us today to egg each other on to goodness.

May 1
World Day of Prayer

The LORD is near to all who call on him, to all who call on him in truth. PSALM 145:18

How many times, Lord, do my children call my name, running through the house yelling for me? Some of these times, I don't even try to answer them because I know they couldn't possibly hear me over the volume of their own voices. And so I wait for them to stop yelling. Help me to remember this today, Lord, when I am praying. Enable me to understand that you might be patiently waiting for me to stop my own yelling. You are waiting for me to listen. Help me to stop talking in my prayer life long enough so that I might actually hear your answer.

MAY 2

Seek the LORD and his strength, seek his presence continually. 1 CHRONICLES 16:11

Some days, Lord, I feel I am continually in the presence of children, clutter, and cartoon characters. And those things are not exactly cornerstones of a strong foundation for a day of great faith in action. Enable me today, dear Lord, to seek you in everything I do. Please enable me to find you in the midst of the chaos.

MAY 3
SAINTS PHILIP AND JAMES, APOSTLES

I will do whatever you ask in my name, so that the Father may be glorified in the Son. If in my name you ask me for anything, I will do it. JOHN 14:13-14

You always want to help people, Jesus. You always want to do the right thing. And yet, you never take the credit, the rewards or the praise for yourself. You continually turn everything back to heaven, to honor the Father. Help me to do good today—to do the right thing. And if by some chance, something good does indeed come out of me today, please enable me to humbly give praise where it is due. I ask this in your heavenly name.

MAY 4

… clothe yourselves with the new self, created
according to the likeness of God in true
righteousness and holiness. EPHESIANS 4:24

Dear God, I know that I put too much
emphasis on how I clothe myself and my
children. How ridiculous this must seem to
you! How absurd it must be to you that we pay
such attention to detail in our outward selves,
and so little attention to the details of our
inward selves! Enable me today to clothe
myself in a way of righteousness and holiness.
And Lord, please help me to know where to
find these very important accessories for my
life.

MAY 5

Pursue peace with everyone, and the holiness without which no one will see the Lord.
HEBREWS 12:14

Peace. Lord, you mention peace so often, I know it has to be so important to you. Some days I know the people in my house need to be reminded that we are to pursue peace with each other. Some days, I need to be reminded, Lord. Please help me today to go out of my way to pursue peace. And when it is hard to find, prompt me to look up to you so that I may see exactly what it is I am searching for.

MAY 6

Even before a word is on my tongue, O LORD, you know it completely. PSALMS 139:4

Lord, forgive me for those words that come off my tongue that do not make you happy. Forgive me for all the words that I seem to shoot off my tongue in anger. It's amazing to think of how well you know me. You know my very words before I ever speak them. Oh, Lord, today, help me to pick out words that are good and loving.

MAY 7

Know therefore that the LORD your God is God.
DEUTERONOMY 7:9

How beautifully simple is the truth that you
are God! You are God. Why do I make it so
difficult? Why do I try to do your job? How
many times do I remind my kids that they are
not the parent, but I am? How many times
must you want to remind me of this wonderful
fact? You are God. You are God.

MAY 8

*Do not let loyalty and faithfulness forsake you; bind
them around your neck, write them on the tablet of
your heart.* PROVERBS 3:3

What do you see written on the tablet of my
heart, Lord? Is it loyalty and faithfulness? Or
do you see pettiness and greed? Today, Lord,
remind me that you can see straight into my
heart. Please help me to erase all that is in my
heart that should not be there. And help me to
write, in the permanent marker my kids always
manage to find, the attributes that will help me
walk closer to you.

MAY 9

So teach us to count our days that we may gain a wise heart. PSALM 90:12

Our days are numbered, aren't they, Lord? None of us is getting any younger. None of us will stay here forever. And yet, we live as if we had all the tomorrows we could possibly dream of. Help me today to start counting the preciousness of each day. Help me to live and love today as if there will be no tomorrow.

MAY 10

So faith comes from what is heard, and what is heard comes through the word of Christ. ROMANS 10:17

Your Word, dear Jesus, is so precious. It is the foundation of faith. It feeds our faith. And yet, you know how long it has been since I last sat down to read your Word. You know the last time I picked up my Bible. You know, but I have forgotten. Please help me today, to start a practice that seeks your Word in my life. Nourish me, dear Lord, with your Word.

MAY 11
MOTHER'S DAY *
(Second Sunday in May)

I delight to do your will, O my God; your law is within my heart. PSALM 40:8

I love being a mom, dear Lord! I really do! You know that some days, I forget to say it. Some days, I feel overwhelmed, exhausted, underpaid and unappreciated. And sometimes those are the good days! But Lord, I love being a mom. Thank you for giving to me the priceless vocation of motherhood.

MAY 12

Happy are those who find wisdom, and those who get understanding. PROVERBS 3:13

Some things I just don't understand, dear Lord. Every time I hear of a child hurting in this world or when I hear of a tragedy reported on the news I wonder why it had to happen. Enable me today to understand what I need to understand and to accept that you, Lord, can handle the rest. And help me please, dear Lord, to know the difference.

MAY 13

The effect of righteousness will be peace, and the result of righteousness, quietness and trust forever.
ISAIAH 32:17

Dear God, what does it mean to be righteous? I hear the word so often, but I can't put my finger on what it really means, Lord. The dictionary says it is "to be holy, devout, or religious." But what does that truly mean? Today, dear Lord, help me to not only be righteous, but also help me to understand with all my heart what it is that you are calling me to be.

MAY 14
SAINT MATTHIAS, THE APOSTLE

O LORD, you know; remember me and visit me…
JEREMIAH 15:15

You know everything, Lord. You know everything. Why do I forget that? Why do I insist on telling you what I think I need? Help me today, dear Lord, to remember that you know! Help me to remember that you remember me.

MAY 15

…we may be mutually encouraged by each other's faith, both yours and mine. ROMANS 1:12

How great it would be, Lord, if we all focused more on being mutually encouraged by each other's faith. Instead, it seems that we are sometimes so caught in the trap of proving why each other's faith is not what it should be. Help me today, to encourage the faith of others and to be encouraged by the faith of others. Remind me to leave the judging of our faith up to you.

MAY 16

My soul thirsts for God, for the living God. When shall I come and behold the face of God? PSALM 42:2

Some days, dear Lord, I feel like I am indeed thirsting. Some days I thirst for stimulating conversation. Some days I thirst for a block of time all to myself. Help me to distinguish between what I merely want and what my soul truly thirsts for. Enable me to quench the thirsts of my soul as you see fit. Remind me to take care of me.

MAY 17

What no eye has seen, nor ear heard, nor the human heart conceived, what God has prepared for those who love him. 1 CORINTHIANS 2:9

Dear God, when I think of each of my newborn babies and the miracles you worked in getting each particular child into my arms at each particular time, I feel I have had a glimpse of your greatness. But it is only a mere glimpse. Remind me today that you have a plan for all who love you. Remind me today that what you have in store for us—the wonder of it all—cannot compare to anything we have ever seen, heard or conceived here on earth.

MAY 18

Enter his gates with thanksgiving, and his courts with praise. Give thanks to him, bless his name. PSALM 100:4

Sometimes, Lord, I feel unappreciated. Some days, I just want to say, "Stop complaining! Can't anyone around here just say thank you?" I will bet you want to say the same to your children. I imagine you get more complaints than compliments. Forgive me Lord, for my ingratitude. Today please help me to enter your gates with thanksgiving and praise—not complaints about being unappreciated.

MAY 19

May the LORD give strength to his people! May the LORD bless his people with peace! PSALM 29:11

Some days, I do feel weak, Lord. Some days I feel physically weak, emotionally weak and spiritually weak. Sometimes I feel like I am looking in all the wrong places to find what I need. I tell myself: "That exercise machine will make me physically stronger or those magazines will make me emotionally stronger or that conference will make me spiritually stronger." Help me today, dear Lord, to stop looking in all the wrong places for my sources of strength. Enable me today to look to you for all my needs.

MAY 20

So if anyone is in Christ, there is a new creation: everything old has passed away; see, everything has become new! 2 CORINTHIANS 5:17

We all come with so much baggage, Lord. There is so much of yesterday that we all try to carry over into tomorrow. Today, please remind me again that all is fresh and pure and new with you. Thank you for making me new again. Help me to leave my baggage in the yesterdays of my past.

MAY 21

As for those who in the present age are rich, command them not to be haughty, or to set their hopes on the uncertainty of riches, but rather on God who richly provides us with everything for our enjoyment. 1 TIMOTHY 6:17

Aren't we such a materialistic society, Lord? We are all victims of the latest ad campaigns telling us what we need. I confess, I want what is new and improved, bigger and better, just as much as the next person. Forgive me this coveting. Rid me of it. Help me today to comprehend that the only riches I should be concerned with are found in a rich, everlasting

life with you. Remind me that your ad
campaign began 2000 years ago.

MAY 22

The joy of the LORD is your strength. NEHEMIAH 8:10

There is such strength in joy, Lord. The
laughter of a child—the pure joyful giggle—
seems to have the power to heal wounds.
Remind me today that this joy is but a hint of
the joy that is to be found in you. Today,
enable me to seek my joy and my strength in
you. Help me, dear Lord, to giggle again.

MAY 23

*As the Father has loved me, so I have loved you;
abide in my love.* JOHN 15:9

You gave us such a good example of love, dear
Jesus. Such a selfless and amazing example!
You lived your life as a lesson in loving.
Remind me today to love as you love. Remind
me today that you loved us to death.

MAY 24

For this is the message you have heard from the beginning, that we should love one another.
1 JOHN 3:11

Love one another. Love one another. Love one another. Lord, you have made it so clear what we are to concentrate on in this life. You did not tell us that we should concentrate on attaining the biggest salaries and the most spacious homes. You never once hinted that fame or fortune was what it was all about. Love one another. You have repeated this message over and over to us all. Please keep repeating it, until everyone in the world knows it by *heart.*

MAY 25

One who gives an honest answer gives a kiss on the lips. PROVERBS 24:26

Honesty. Dear God, I would like to pretend that I am honest. I tell myself I am honest because I don't steal and I don't cheat. But, Lord, is it honest to fib to the person on the phone who is trying to sell me something? Is it okay that I make up a story when I think the truth will hurt someone—or me? Please help

me today to practice being honest. Gently call
my attention to the times when my mouth is
not being true to my heart.

MAY 26
ASCENSION THURSDAY*

*So then the Lord Jesus, after he had spoken to them,
was taken up into heaven and sat down at the right
hand of God.* MARK 16:19

Was it hard to leave that day, Lord? You knew
how weak everyone was. You knew how hard
it would be for those left behind to carry your
Gospel into the world. Did you ever think
about staying a few more days—a few more
years? I have a hard time entrusting my
children to do their chores without me
constantly being present. How did you have
such incredible faith in the people who had
already let you down? Was it simply that you
knew they had incredible faith in you?

MAY 27

If God is for us, who is against us? ROMANS 8:31

God, I know that you are omnipotent. I know
that you are omniscient. I know that you are
everywhere. But still I worry. Still I fear. Today,
dear God, please fill my heart with the
complete knowledge that you are all the things
I know you are. Fill me with the complete
understanding that if you are for me, who can
be against me?

MAY 28

*I took courage, for the hand of the LORD my God
was upon me.* EZRA 7:28

Lord, there have been times in my life when I
truly felt your hand on me. Those times were
so precious to me. But there have been times
when I wondered where you were. I couldn't
find you. Today remind me that if you are not
with me, I am the one to blame. I am the one
who moved. Please keep me close, Lord. Let
me feel your hand on me today.

MAY 29

May those who sow in tears reap with shouts of joy. PSALM 126:5

Lord, it is so hard for us to understand suffering. It is hard for us to rejoice in suffering. And there is so much pain and suffering these days. Today, I pray for all who are sick and suffering in any way. Help them where they need it most. Help them to see their tears finally turn to shouts of joy.

MAY 30
MEMORIAL DAY*
(4th Monday of May)

Now the Lord is the Spirit, and where the Spirit of the Lord is, there is freedom. 2 CORINTHIANS 3:17

So much thought and consideration is given to freedom today, Lord. We talk about freedom from persecution. We talk about freedom of speech, freedom for ours and other countries. Help us today to give thanks for those people who have given their lives for our freedom. But enable us, too, dear Jesus, to give thanks to you today for the freedom from sin for which you gave your life.

MAY 31
VISITATION OF MARY

When Elizabeth heard Mary's greeting, the child leaped in her womb. And Elizabeth was filled with the Holy Spirit and exclaimed with a loud cry, "Blessed are you among women, and blessed is the fruit of your womb." LUKE 1:41–42

It's amazing, Mary. John the Baptist, who wasn't even born yet, leapt in his mother's womb, because he recognized the Lord in yours. And yet, every day, we see Christ around us in so many ways, and we forget to leap for joy. Sometimes we don't even recognize him. As his mother, this must hurt you greatly. Forgive us for our complacency. Forgive us for not leaping for joy every time we feel the presence of your son, Jesus Christ. Remind us, dear Blessed Mother, to daily leap for joy and proclaim how blessed the fruit of your womb truly is.

JUNE 1

Then Job answered the LORD: "See, I am of small account; what shall I answer you? I lay my hand on my mouth." JOB 40:3-4

Dear God, you know that there are many times throughout my day when I need to acknowledge that I am of small account. Too many days, I confess, my ego gets fed from the position of power that I have from being a mom. I like feeling like I am in charge. I like making decisions for my family. But please remind me today, God, that I am not in charge. I am not in control. I may happen to be the earthly mother, but I am not the Heavenly Father.

June 2

Now the man knew his wife Eve, and she conceived and bore Cain, saying, "I have produced a man with the help of the Lord." Genesis 4:1

Lord, when you create a baby, you create a miracle. If you did nothing else but create babies, I would still need to praise you for all my life. But Lord, you create the tiniest finger of a newborn with the same hand that created the enormity of the world. Today, Lord, help me to see your amazing hand everywhere I go. Help me to stop taking your precious miracles for granted.

June 3

. . . the Lord make his face to shine upon you, and be gracious to you. Numbers 6:25

Oh, Lord, shine your face upon me today. Help me to truly feel you in the sunshine. Remind me to stop somewhere along the course of my busy day for just a moment and completely allow you to shine upon me. Let me feel you shining, Lord. Today let me feel the warmth of your face shining upon me.

JUNE 4

So have no fear; I myself will provide for you and your little ones. GENESIS 50:21

Why do I worry, Lord? Why do I always have fear and anxiety about something? Will there be enough time to do what needs to be done? Will there be enough food to feed everyone? Will there be enough money at the end of the month? Does it hurt you when I worry like that? Does it insult you that I must not trust you enough? Please forgive me, Lord. Take away my worries. Help me to have no fear.

JUNE 5

...he will love you, bless you, and multiply you; he will bless the fruit of your womb and the fruit of your ground, your grain and your wine and your oil, the increase of your cattle and the issue of your flock. DEUTERONOMY 7:13

Lord, we live in a world where things that sound too good to be true usually are. We have been raised to doubt claims that promise us anything at all. But you have promised us everything. You have promised that you will take care of us here and for eternity. You have promised us the world, if we believe. Help us today to believe that you are too good and you are true.

JUNE 6

Talk no more so very proudly, let not arrogance come from your mouth; for the LORD is a God of knowledge, and by him actions are weighed. 1 SAMUEL 2:3

If you weighed my actions yesterday, Lord, what did you see? Was the scale leaning on the side of goodness, or on the side of sinfulness? And when something good tipped the scale onto the side of goodness, did I get so boastful and proud that the scale tipped back towards the sinful side? Please help me today, dear Lord, to remember that you are weighing my actions. Please help me to balance my life toward the side of goodness.

JUNE 7

Again, if two lie together, they keep warm; but how can one keep warm alone? ECCLESIASTES 4:11-16

Dear Jesus, you know that there are a lot of lonely people in this world. And some of the lonely people actually live in a house full of others, but still they are so alone. Help us today to remember we need each other. Enable us today to reach out to those who might be feeling alone. Help us to find the warmth of your love in each other.

JUNE 8
PENTECOST*
(50 Days after Easter)

For the promise is for you, for your children, and for all who are far away, everyone whom the Lord our God calls to him. ACTS 2:39

You are calling us all, aren't you, Lord? Some days we act as if you are only calling a few people to be with you. We act as if you are calling the people already in your churches, already on their knees. But you are calling everyone, near and far. Help me today, dear Lord, to help spread your call throughout my home and my community. And help me to hear you calling me today as well.

JUNE 9

This is my comfort in my distress, that your promise gives me life. PSALM 119:50

Dear God, you gave me life. You gave me life! I need to say that sometimes in order to truly understand the impact of the reality. You gave me life. You gave my family life. You gave us all life. Thank you for life, dear Father in heaven.

JUNE 10

And Jesus increased in wisdom and in years, and in divine and human favor. LUKE 2:52

Lord Jesus, the Bible gives a one-sentence account of close to twenty years of your young life. All we are told about you after you are in the temple until you are an adult is that you grew in wisdom and in years. We blink, and you are grown. Help me to realize that that rapid pace is happening with my own children. Soon I will blink and they will be grown. Help me to make this time worthy so that they too may be growing in wisdom as well as in years.

JUNE 11

You shall not take vengeance or bear a grudge against any of your people, but you shall love your neighbor as yourself: I am the LORD. LEVITICUS 19:18

Dear Lord, how many times do I ask you to forgive me for something? How many times do I recognize I have been wrong and ask forgiveness from you? And I know you are loving and merciful, and you will forgive me. But, likewise, how many times do I hold a grudge against someone else? How many times do I not forgive? Today, dear Lord, help me to truly forgive the person I need to forgive the most. Help me to love the person in my life who I feel might deserve it the least.

JUNE 12

O give thanks to the LORD, for he is good; for his steadfast love endures forever. 1 CHRONICLES 16:34

Have I thanked you yet today, dear Lord? Did I thank you for getting us all through another night? Did I thank you for keeping us safe throughout the day? Did I praise you for every breath you allowed us to take? Forgive me for forgetting to be grateful for or not recognizing

the wonderful blessings you give us every day.
And Lord, thank you. Thank you.

JUNE 13

*Are not two sparrows sold for a penny? Yet not one
of them will fall to the ground apart from your
Father.* MATTHEW 10:29

Sometimes Lord, we moms seem to have eyes
in the back of our heads. We see more than
our children think we see. And yet even we
forget how your eye is on everything you
made. You see everything at all times. Your eye
is, indeed, on the sparrow, but somehow you're
watching the rest of us cuckoo birds as well.

JUNE 14

And even the hairs of your head are all counted.
MATTHEW 10:30

Lord, I can confidently trust you with the big things in my life: my faith, my home, my children. I rest secure in the knowledge that you are taking care of the big things. But, I confess, dear Lord, I worry about the details. I get anxious over the little things that I think you won't want to bother about. Remind me that you pay attention to details, too. Help me to see that you are big enough to be in the small things, too.

JUNE 15
FATHER'S DAY*
(3rd Sunday in June)

Honor your father and mother… MATTHEW 19:19

Sometimes, dear God, I forget to recognize the importance of my children's father in their lives. I get so caught up with my role of mommy that I lose sight of how vital daddy is to them as well. Help me today to try harder to value my children's father more and more. Help me to teach my children to honor their father by honoring him myself.

...do not fear, for I am with you, do not be afraid, for I am your God; I will strengthen you, I will help you, I will uphold you with my victorious right hand. ISAIAH 41:10

Dear God, on the very first day of school, when I had to put my firstborn on that big bus and watch the door slam shut taking her where I could not go, I was so afraid. Part of me wished I could go with her to protect her throughout her day. I know, though, I cannot be everywhere she goes. But you can, dear Lord. You are always there. Wherever our loved ones are, wherever we are, so too, are you.

JUNE 17

I have not hidden your saving help within my heart,
I have spoken of your faithfulness and your
salvation; I have not concealed your steadfast love
and your faithfulness from the great congregation.
PSALM 40:10

Dear Jesus, sometimes I am guilty of hiding
your love in my heart. I know you love me and
I love you. But sometimes, I keep it to myself.
I forget about the importance of sharing it with
others. Forgive me for this greediness. Enable
me today to understand that the best way to
thank you for your love for me is to share it
with everyone I meet. Help me, Lord, to do
just that.

JUNE 18

For you were called to freedom, brothers and sisters;
only do not use your freedom as an opportunity for
self-indulgence, but through love become slaves to
one another. GALATIANS 5:13

Lord, some days I do feel like I am a slave to
my family. All I do is serve them. But you say
that is good. We should spend our lives
serving each other. But does my work count
for goodness if I serve with a heart that is not

happy to serve? If I am mumbling about being unappreciated as I fix them dinner, does it still make you happy, Lord? Please help me today to delight in serving my family. Enable me to serve with a glad heart. And please, every once in a while, enable someone to serve me as well.

JUNE 19

Nevertheless, some good is found in you, for you have set your heart to seek God. 2 CHRONICLES 19:3

Lord, I want my heart to always be set to seek you. But I confess that some days my heart is preoccupied with more self-centered quests. Some days my heart seeks a moment alone. Some days my heart seeks peace and quiet among the chaos. Help me today to truly set my heart to seek you. May you find some good in me today.

JUNE 20

Hannah prayed and said, "My heart exults in the LORD; my strength is exalted in my God."
1 SAMUEL 2:1

On some of my busiest days, Lord, my body parts seem to cry out to me. My head pounds from the noise of the day. My back aches from the little ones I carry. My voice gives out from giving too many commands. But even on those days, dear Lord, help my heart to cry out in joy for you. Enable my heart to exult in you. Help me to find in you, dear Lord, the strength I need to make it through my day with all my parts intact.

JUNE 21

You do well if you really fulfill the royal law according to the scripture, "You shall love your neighbor as yourself." JAMES 2:8

Dear God, do you think I do really well fulfilling any of your laws? I know that I am fine with keeping some of them all the time. But I realize I only keep others of them some of the time. Help me today, dear Lord, to keep your laws with the same consistency that you love me—all the time.

JUNE 22
BODY AND BLOOD OF CHRIST

The cup of blessing that we bless, is it not a sharing in the blood of Christ? The bread that we break, is it not a sharing in the body of Christ? 1 CORINTHIANS 10:16

Thank you, Lord Jesus, for the gift of life you give to me at every Mass. Thank you, for the daily offering to me of your body and blood through the Eucharist. Enable me today to accept your precious gift as I have never accepted it before.

JUNE 23

The LORD is near to the brokenhearted, and saves the crushed in spirit. PSALM 34:18

Today, Lord, I know I might pass someone who is brokenhearted. Somewhere close to me, there may be someone who is crushed in spirit. Whether these people might be my family and friends, or complete strangers to me, allow me today, dear Lord, to be your eyes and see their pain. Help me to help others. Help me to bring you to others in need.

JUNE 24
SAINT JOHN THE BAPTIST

I baptize you with water for repentance, but one who is more powerful than I is coming after me; I am not worthy to carry his sandals. He will baptize you with the Holy Spirit and fire. MATTHEW 3:11

I am not worthy, dear Lord. The great John the Baptist was wise enough to proclaim his unworthiness and yet we sometimes forget to acknowledge our own unworthiness when it comes to you. Thank you for coming for me, loving me, dying for me, even though I am not worthy. Thank you, Lord.

JUNE 25

How can we thank God enough for you in return for all the joy that we feel before our God because of you? 1 THESSALONIANS 3:9

God, how can I thank you enough? How can I thank you enough for the little ones that make my life somewhat sticky and messy and exhausting, and yet so very wonderful? How can I thank you enough, dear God? How can I ever thank you enough?

JUNE 26

Hatred stirs up strife, but love covers all offenses.
PROVERBS 10:12

Lord, I hate the word *hate*. It has always been such an ugly word to me. Help me to continually keep it from the mouths of my children. Better yet, help me to continually keep it from the hearts of my children. Help us today, dear Lord, to love that word away.

JUNE 27
SACRED HEART OF JESUS*
(3rd Friday after Pentecost)

"Which of these three, do you think, was a neighbor to the man who fell into the hands of the robbers?" He said, "The one who showed him mercy." Jesus said to him, "Go and do likewise." LUKE 10:36-37

Dear Lord, we moms have a reputation for repeatedly instructing our kids to share. "It's nice to share. Sharing is caring." And yet I have to wonder if I am giving them a good example of sharing every day. Do my children see me sharing? Help me today, dear Lord, to be a good example of sharing love. Enable me to share your Sacred Heart with others.

JUNE 28

Hear the word that the LORD speaks to you.
JEREMIAH 10:1

Lord, do you have something to say to me, today? Are you speaking to me now? Am I even listening to you? It's hard to listen, Lord, when there is so much noise all around me. But sometimes, the loudest noise I hear is, admittedly, my own voice. Today, dear Lord, please enable me to hear your voice over all the other noises of my day.

JUNE 29
SAINTS PETER AND PAUL

Then Peter came and said to him, "Lord, if another member of the church sins against me, how often should I forgive? As many as seven times?" Jesus said to him, "Not seven times, but, I tell you, seventy-seven times." MATTHEW 18:21-22

Little ones are so forgiving, Lord. They might easily get their feelings hurt, but as soon as they receive an apology, they are playing their games together again. We adults don't do that as well, do we, Lord? Help me today to learn

from my children how to forgive and forget
and how to keep on playing this game of life
with a happy heart.

June 30

*From there you will seek the L*ORD *your God, and
you will find him if you search after him with all
your heart and soul.* DEUTERONOMY 4:29

Sometimes, Lord, my children are looking for
something that is right under their noses.
Sometimes they get so caught up in the
searching that they don't recognize that which
they seek. Aren't we all like that when it comes
to you, Lord? Do we too often look high and
low for you, unable to see that you are right
beside us the entire time? Help me to seek you
constantly today. And please, Lord, enable me
to recognize you in my search.

JULY 1

In the beginning was the Word, and the Word was with God, and the Word was God. JOHN 1:1

My dear Jesus, when you came you brought us everything we truly need. Everything. You came to bring us life. With no thought to your own self, you came so that we could live. How it must hurt you when we disappoint you with our sin and our greed and our selfishness. Help me to live better today than I did yesterday. Enable me to walk more directly in the light of your word.

JULY 2

For nothing will be impossible with God. LUKE 1:37

How many impossibilities have you made possible today, Lord? How many miracles have you worked in my life during the last twenty-four hours? And how many times have I failed to notice these wonders? Forgive me today for the many times I overlook your majestic hand as it touches my life. Forgive me for ever taking for granted the fact that nothing is impossible with you.

JULY 3
SAINT THOMAS, APOSTLE

Jesus said to him, "Have you believed because you have seen me? Blessed are those who have not seen and yet have come to believe." JOHN 20:29

Lord, I am a doubter, just like Thomas. I am a skeptic. I need to touch, feel and see things with my own hands and eyes before I fully believe. And yet, so much of faith is based on believing what we do not see. Today, dear Lord, please help me to overcome any doubts I possess concerning my faith. Enable me to have the passionate faith of a trusting child.

JULY 4
INDEPENDENCE DAY

You shall eat your fill and bless the LORD your God for the good land that he has given you. DEUTERONOMY 8:10

It all comes from you, dear God. It all comes from you. And yet we forget this too often. We feel ownership in our land, our country, our families, even in our very own lives. And yet it all comes from you. Help me today as I celebrate the Independence of America to also remember to rejoice in my dependence on you.

JULY 5

*Therefore confess your sins to one another, and pray
for one another, so that you may be healed. The
prayer of the righteous is powerful and effective.*
JAMES 5:16

Dear God, I like discussing faith with the
people from my church. And it feels so right to
pray with the people from my prayer group.
But Lord, how am I doing with discussing faith
with my children? How am I doing with
teaching them to pray, truly pray? Help me
today to be a mother who truly lives her faith.
Enable us all to raise faith-filled families.

JULY 6

*Do not be deceived: "Bad company ruins good
morals."* 1 CORINTHIANS 15:33

Lord, we moms are always telling our children
to make wise choices in the company they
keep. And yet sometimes we overlook the
company that is coming to them through their
radios, televisions and computers. And, dear
Lord, so many things out there sadden and
frighten me. Enable me today to be a wise

mother. Guide me to instill in my children good morals. Help me, please, to help them to naturally seek good company.

July 7

But Peter and the apostles answered, "We must obey God rather than any human authority." Acts 5:29

Dear Lord, forgive us for lifting some people up too high. We really get confused with whom we adore, don't we? Help me today to admire people who have achieved admirable goals. But enable me to keep from looking to them for the goals of my life. Remind me to only worship you.

JULY 8

Bear one another's burdens, and in this way you will fulfill the law of Christ. GALATIANS 6:2

Dear God, I know that into every life a little rain must fall. Please help me today to build up those vital lines of communication with my family. Enable me to secure these lifelines when the sun is shining on us so that when the rain falls, we will be able and willing to bear each other's burdens. And remind me that you are asking me to keep those same lines of communication built up with you, dear Father, rain or shine.

JULY 9

…not neglecting to meet together, as is the habit of some, but encouraging one another, and all the more as you see the Day approaching. HEBREWS 10:25

Dear Lord, it is so easy to find excuses not to go to Mass. Busy schedules, late nights, sporting events. We must disappoint you so much when all we hear is the world calling us, and we ignore your call. Fortify me today to commit to good habits of worship. Help me to set a good example of churchgoing for my

family. Please make it impossible for me to
ignore your call.

JULY 10

*Again Jesus spoke to them, saying, "I am the light of
the world. Whoever follows me will never walk in
darkness but will have the light of life."* JOHN 8:12

Dear Jesus, I take it for granted that I nightly
walk into a dark room and turn on a light
switch. The brilliant flash of light that fills the
room is an expected part of my life. And yet,
still, it is so amazing. This is what you do for
the world, dear Lord. You fill the darkness of
the world with brilliant light. You are the Light
of the World. Enable me today to fully
embrace this blessing, never taking it for
granted. Enable me today to completely walk
in the light with you.

JULY 11

And we are witnesses to these things, and so is the Holy Spirit whom God has given to those who obey him. ACTS 5:32

How, dear Lord, can anyone who has ever witnessed the birth of a child deny you? How can anyone look at a new and perfect life beginning with the sound of a tiny cry, and not fall to their knees with praise and thanksgiving? You have blessed our lives with these gifts of love and hope and joy. Help us today to bless the lives of those we meet by willingly sharing those gifts of the Holy Spirit with them as well.

JULY 12

Let no evil talk come out of your mouths, but only what is useful for building up, as there is need, so that your words may give grace to those who hear. EPHESIANS 4:29

Lord, if you took away all the words I said yesterday that were not useful for building up, would I have any words left at all? Forgive me for all the idleness and gossip that comes out of my mouth. Strengthen me, today, so that I might do a better job at watching my words.

Remind me, please, that my little ones are watching . . . and learning from me.

JULY 13

And this is the testimony: God gave us eternal life, and this life is in his Son. Whoever has the Son has life; whoever does not have the Son of God does not have life. 1 JOHN 5:11-12

It's pretty simple, isn't it Jesus? If we have you in our life, we have eternal life. And if we don't have you in our life, we don't have eternal life. Why is this so hard for us to understand? And why, even after we get the main idea, is it so hard to stay focused on such a basic truth? Forgive me, Lord, for the many times my words have claimed to have you in my life but my actions prove otherwise. Help me today to plant you so deeply in my life that my actions will always be affected by your merciful presence.

JULY 14
BLESSED KATERI TEKAKWITHA

Who will teach me what is agreeable to God that I may do it? SAINT KATERI TEKAKWITHA

Dear Lord, help me to hear my children's voices in this thought from the first Native American woman—as well as the first North American laywoman—to be beatified. As Blessed Kateri so beautifully expressed, help me to sense that my children will always ask of me, "Who will teach me what is agreeable to God?" Help me, Lord, to daily volunteer for the job of teaching them. And help me to teach them through actions even more than words.

JULY 15

One does not live by bread alone, but by every word that comes from the mouth of God. MATTHEW 4:4

Sometimes I am guilty, dear God, of pretending that I live on bread alone. I pay so much attention to the material things for my family—the food on the table, the clothes in the closets, the house that we live in—that I run out of time to pay attention to you at all.

I run out of time to listen to your Word. Forgive me, please, God. Enable me to hear your words again in my life. Help me to take the time to listen, before I really do run out of time.

July 16

Through him, then, let us continually offer a sacrifice of praise to God, that is, the fruit of lips that confess his name. HEBREWS 13:15

Some days, dear Lord, I feel my heart praises you continually. I feel your love deep within me. But am I doing okay with getting this praise to come out my lips? Do I talk of your love to others often enough? Truthfully, I suspect I could never talk of the wonders of your love often enough. Guide me today, dear Jesus, to seek opportunities to praise you and thank you with my lips as well as my heart.

JULY 17

He must increase, but I must decrease. JOHN 3:30

Dear Jesus, our world is set up on the belief that bigger is better. We must increase in wealth and power and importance in order to be worth anything. And yet this is the opposite of what you tell us. You tell us less is more. Remind me today that if I am full of myself, there will be no room for you. Help me to lose myself today by finding you.

JULY 18

No testing has overtaken you that is not common to everyone. God is faithful, and he will not let you be tested beyond your strength, but with the testing he will also provide the way out so that you may be able to endure it. 1 CORINTHIANS 10:13

Dear God, Mother Teresa once said she knew you would never give her anything she couldn't handle—but sometimes she wished you didn't have such confidence in her. Help me today to accept the testing that you have in store for me with an open heart. Enable me to learn and grow in the direction you have set for me. But I know I am weak, Lord. Please remind me of these brave words over and over

again while the testing is going on. Help me to
feel you with me, over and over again.

JULY 19

*All scripture is inspired by God and is useful for
teaching, for reproof, for correction, and for training
in righteousness.* 2 TIMOTHY 3:16

Before I had my first child, dear God, I must
have read ten books on pregnancy and
parenting. Since that time, the list continues to
grow. I want to learn all I can about this most
important job. But I confess, Lord, that I do
not often enough open the book that could
help me the most with motherhood. I do not
read my Bible as I should. Help me to turn to
your sacred Word to find the true answers that
I seek. Please put it in my heart to start today.

July 20

I hereby command you: Be strong and courageous; do not be frightened or dismayed, for the LORD your God is with you wherever you go. JOSHUA 1:9

Lord, I do know you are with me wherever I go. And yet, still I get frightened at times. My head can comprehend that it does not make sense to ever be afraid if I truly know you are with me. But my heart sometimes does fear. Help me today, dear Lord, to know you are with me so completely that I feel it through and through. Help me to know it with all my heart.

July 21

Until now you have not asked for anything in my name. Ask and you will receive, so that your joy may be complete. JOHN 16:24

One of my greatest prayers for my children is that they will be happy, Lord. I want joy to fill their lives. This must be your desire for your children. You want us to be happy. You want joy to fill our lives. How it must hurt you when we suffer in silence, not bringing our fears and our worries to you. Guide me today, dear Lord, to tell you all that is in my heart. Help me, please, to find complete joy in you.

JULY 22

It is the spirit that gives life; the flesh is useless. The words that I have spoken to you are spirit and life. JOHN 6:63

We worry so much about the flesh, don't we Lord? There are million-dollar industries thriving on our obsessions with the flesh. And I know I need to let go of these obsessions, too. Help me today to spend less time worrying about the physical things in my life so that I have more time to focus on the spiritual things of life. Remind me that if I grip my material possessions too tightly, it will become impossible for me to still cling to you.

JULY 23

…and it is no longer I who live, but it is Christ who lives in me. And the life I now live in the flesh I live by faith in the Son of God, who loved me and gave himself for me. GALATIANS 2:20

Guide me today, dear God, to remember it is not about my life as much as it is about you living in me. You live in me! Talk about your fixer-upper! I need so much work, Lord. Help me today to begin to remodel my life so that it might be more worthy of you.

JULY 24

For he will command his angels concerning you to guard you in all your ways. PSALM 91:11

Thank you, Lord, for the angels that you send to protect us, guide us, or simply cheer us when we are down. So many times when I am in need, someone says something or does something that really makes a difference. And whether these angels have wings and halos or jeans and baseball caps does not matter. All I need to know is that they are sent from you. Thank you, Lord.

JULY 25
SAINT JAMES, APOSTLE

And he said to them, "Follow me, and I will make you fish for people." MATTHEW 4:19

Help me today, dear Lord, to truly fish for people for your kingdom. Please encourage me to start with my own children. Enable me daily to gather them for you in a net of love. Help me use patience and gentleness as bait. Guide me in your ways so that I may never lose any of this precious catch. And may none ever be thrown back.

JULY 26
SAINTS JOACHIM AND ANNE

But he knows the way that I take; when he has tested me, I shall come out like gold. JOB 23:10

No one looks forward to a test, dear God. Every time one of my children has a scheduled test at school, we spend a lot of time the night before studying so that the end result will be better. But what studying should I do to prepare me for the tests that you plan for me? Should I pace my studying? Or do I need to cram for this upcoming exam? Please help me with this, Lord. I want to pass these tests of life.

JULY 27

O sing to the LORD a new song; sing to the LORD, all the earth. PSALM 96:1

Someone once said that singing is praying twice. If that is the case, Lord, please allow me to fill my house with singing today. Not with rock or rap music, but guide me to fill it with songs of praise to you. Only you could turn a house full of sinners into a houseful of singers.

JULY 28

Sing to the LORD, bless his name; tell of his salvation from day to day. PSALM 96:2

Dear Lord, when my husband and I first met, I could not stop talking about him to everyone I came into contact with. It is natural to desire to share thoughts of love with others. But do I share the love I feel for you with others? Have I lately had any conversations where I tell of the love you have for us all? Today, dear Lord, empower me to tell everyone of your love. Help me to sing this love song to all I meet.

JULY 29

Keep your heart with all vigilance, for from it flow the springs of life. PROVERBS 4:23

Lord, you know we do a decent job of guarding our material possessions. We have insurance policies for our houses and our cars. We have the best locks and security systems money can buy. And yet, we so often forget to guard and protect our hearts. Too many times, we allow them to become damaged with sin. Help me today, dear Lord, to cleanse my heart of all that should not be in it. And guide me to keep it that way. Remind me that having your love in my heart is the best insurance I can ever have.

Bless the LORD, O my soul, and all that is within me, bless his holy name. PSALM 103:1

How awesome you are, God! When I think of all you have done for me—all you continue to do for me—I am amazed. All I have to do is look at each of my children—each a beautiful blend of personalities, temperaments, looks and talents, but each one so very different from the other— and I want to marvel at your majestic manner. I want to bless your holy name, dear Lord.

JULY 31
SAINT IGNATIUS LOYOLA

Everything that one turns in the direction of God is a prayer. SAINT IGNATIUS OF LOYOLA

Sometimes, dear God, all my children have to do is look at me a certain way and I know they are hurting. I can tell they need to talk. How much greater, dear Lord, is your ability to know when your children are hurting—when we are in need? Help me today to learn from the inspirational Saint Ignatius, who taught us so much about prayer. Remind me today that all I have to do at any given time is turn to my Father and talk.

AUGUST 1
SAINT ALPHONSE LIGOURI

For from him and through him and to him are all things. To him be the glory forever. Amen.
ROMANS 11:36

From you . . . through you . . . to you. That pretty much sums it up, doesn't it, Lord? Our life is a gift from you. We only live through you. We hope to one day come to you. Today, dear Jesus, when my thoughts get complicated and I start to think too many things, whisper to me the simple truth that it is all from you . . . through you . . . to you.

AUGUST 2

Do to others as you would have them do to you.
LUKE 6:31

Lord, it seems lately we are raising a generation to believe that the rule to follow is, "Do unto others before they do unto you." Help me today to instill in my children the commandment of being kind to others, treating them as we want to be treated. Enable me today to do a better job of modeling this behavior for them than I did yesterday.

AUGUST 3

The LORD will fulfill his purpose for me; your steadfast love, O LORD, endures forever. Do not forsake the work of your hands. PSALM 138:8

Dear God, so many times I hear of parents who get fed up with ungrateful or unruly children. They simply cannot take it anymore. But you, dear God, you never get fed up. Even though you have every right to forsake us all, you don't give up on us. Help me today to remember this merciful fact. Empower me today to never give up on my children or you.

AUGUST 4

Beloved, do not believe every spirit, but test the spirits to see whether they are from God; for many false prophets have gone out into the world. 1 JOHN 4:1

It is hard, Lord, to know whether something is from you, from the world or from somewhere else. Sometimes I feel I know what you are telling me to do and I am confident it is your will for me. Other times, I think I am acting on your will, but it turns out to be my own thoughts. Help me today to distinguish your Holy Spirit from unholy spirits.

AUGUST 5

Blessed are you who are poor, for yours is the kingdom of God. LUKE 6:20

Dear God, why is it that every time my family struggles with money issues, we don't feel blessed? Why, when I balance my checkbook, do I not feel particularly chosen by you? I know that the best things in life are free. But the fact remains that a lot of really important stuff costs money. Help me with this, today, dear Lord. Empower me to control my finances without being controlled by them.

AUGUST 6
TRANSFIGURATION OF JESUS

Then Peter said to Jesus, "Rabbi, it is good for us to be here; let us make three dwellings, one for you, one for Moses, and one for Elijah." MARK 9:5

Lord, when I have been to a special spiritual retreat or conference, I feel like Peter felt on that mountaintop. I never want to leave. I want to stay there and continue to be filled by your Holy Spirit. But you have not called me to a cloistered life. You have called me to a life of being a mother, among many other roles. You call me to go back home. Help me to fill up with your Holy Spirit enough on those special occasions that I can go back home with a happy heart that has no choice but to share your spirit with everyone in my life.

AUGUST 7

The discerning person looks to wisdom, but the eyes of a fool to the ends of the earth. PROVERBS 17:24

My dear Lord, when I first became a parent, I looked for wisdom. I wanted to learn every thing I could. I realized how little I knew about being a mom. After a while, I would start to figure it out. And then things would change so that I once again had so much to learn. Help me to recognize that this pattern of constantly growing and changing and learning has to be present in my spiritual life as well. Help me to always seek to learn more about you. Keep me today, dear Lord, from being a fool and thinking that I already know what I need to know.

AUGUST 8
SAINT DOMINIC

But strive first for the kingdom of God and his righteousness, and all these things will be given to you as well. MATTHEW 6:33

Forgive me, Lord. Too many times, I forget to put you first. I spend so much of my day striving for material things—all the things the world tells me I need. And too many times, I leave my thoughts of you as an afterthought. Help me today to seek you first in my life. May you be my first thought in the morning, Lord, and my last one at night.

AUGUST 9

The LORD has done great things for us, and we rejoiced. PSALM 126:3

Thank you, Lord! Thank you, Lord! Thank you, Lord! I will never—on this earth—be able to comprehend the magnificently merciful deeds you have done for me. And yet, still I pray that today you allow me to start trying to say "Thank you"—not just with my mouth—but also with my whole being. Thank you, Lord!

*The LORD God has given me the tongue of a teacher,
that I may know how to sustain the weary with a
word. Morning by morning he wakens—wakens my
ear to listen as those who are taught.* ISAIAH 50:4

Dear God, what came off my tongue yesterday?
Was it words that would help lift and sustain a
weary world? Or were my words more along
the lines of those that add deadweight to a
sinking ship? Forgive me, please, Lord, for the
many times I waste my words. Forgive my
tongue for not always teaching, as a mother
should. Forgive my ear for not always listening
as those who are taught.

August 11
Saint Clare

They say that we are too poor, but can a heart which possesses the infinite God be truly poor?
SAINT CLARE

Dear Lord, please allow me today to learn from the loving spirit of Saint Clare. Help me to discover the pure joy she felt in helping others. Enable me today to comprehend how a woman born to a life of privilege could willingly and happily give up everything to follow you. Help me, Lord, to give up my desire for possessing anything other than you.

August 12

For I know that my Redeemer lives, and that at the last he will stand upon the earth. JOB 19:25

Dear Jesus, you are, indeed, my redeemer. Truthfully, I had to look up that word, because I usually only use it when I am talking about coupons. But the dictionary tells me that a redeemer is one who saves, delivers, or rescues someone or something. And that is what you did for me. You saved me. You delivered me.

You rescued me. Thank you, Lord. Help me today to tell the world that I live only because my redeemer lives.

AUGUST 13

All things came into being through him, and without him not one thing came into being. What has come into being in him was life, and the life was the light of all people. JOHN 1:3-4

How can anyone not believe in you, my dear Lord? How can anyone deny that you gave us life? I can only imagine how painful it would be if one of my children turned to me one day and said, "You are not my mother!" How it must hurt you infinitely more to have given life to your children only to have so many reject you. What can I do today to help with that, Lord? What can I do today to help you?

AUGUST 14
SAINT MAXIMILIAN KOLBE

The most deadly poison of our time is indifference.
SAINT MAXIMILIAN KOLBE

Dear Lord, I want to help the hungry of the world, but first I have to fix dinner for my family. I want to relieve the homeless situation, but first I need to clean my house. Forgive me Lord. In my busy-ness, I have become indifferent. In my concern for my children, I have forgotten to help all of your children. Show me today where I can begin to make a difference instead of simply being indifferent.

AUGUST 15
ASSUMPTION OF MARY

And Mary said, "My soul magnifies the Lord."
LUKE 1:46

Dear Mother Mary, you always have the right attitude. No matter what was going on in your life and no matter what you were being called to do, you did it and you did it well. And what is more, you never accepted the glory for yourself, rather you offered it all to the Lord. Help me, Mary, to have a better attitude. Enable me to do well whatever I am being called

to do, offering the glory to God. Help me,
please, to learn about being a mom from you.

AUGUST 16

*Not to us, O LORD, not to us, but to your name give
glory, for the sake of your steadfast love and your
faithfulness.* PSALM 115:1

Dear God, we build million-dollar sports
arenas to honor our sports stars. We walk
around in clothing that tells the name of our
favorite superstar. We pay billions to ordinary
people who we have decided deserve to be
famous. And yet we hesitate to give extra
money to build a new church. We don't want
to push our religion on others by boldly
wearing our religious symbols. We forget to
give glory to you, oh Lord. Help me today to
remember to focus my glorious praise and
adulation where it truly belongs.

Be faithful until death, and I will give you the crown of life. REVELATION 2:10

Dear God, some days, I would love to have a crown. I want a crown that says, *Super Mom* or *World's Best Mom*. But the demanding job of motherhood does not come with those kinds of rewards. No, I'm not going to get a crown for being a mom. But you have promised me a crown of life simply for loving you. Help me to earn this reward, dear Lord. Please enable this crown to go to my head.

Blessed are those who hunger and thirst for righteousness, for they will be filled. MATTHEW 5:6

Lord, most days, I am surrounded by hungry and thirsty people. Most days it seems all I do is clean up my kitchen just in time for the next meal or snack to begin. Today, dear Lord, as I work to fill my children with food and drink to keep them healthy and happy in this life, help me to put effort also into giving them food for their souls that will help them be healthy and happy forever. Remind me that spiritual nourishment is vital for them. And what's more, it won't mess up my kitchen.

AUGUST 19

When Christ who is your life is revealed, then you also will be revealed with him in glory.
COLOSSIANS 3:4

Dear Jesus, when you are revealed, will I be next to you? Or will I be watching from far away? Will I be singing songs of praise for you? Or will I be unable to speak at all? Will I recognize you right away? Or will you be slowly revealed to me? There is so much I don't know about that incredible day, dear Jesus. But this I do know: I love you. And I can't wait to meet you.

AUGUST 20
SAINT BERNARD

God should be loved without thought of reward.
SAINT BERNARD

Dear God, some times when I grant my
children a favor or request, they say, "Thank
you! I love you!" At these times, I am happy to
make them happy, but I want to remind them
that love is unconditional. It is not based on
what someone gets out of a relationship. But
do I do that to you, Lord? Do I tell you most
often that I love you after my prayer has been
answered? Forgive me for that, Lord. Remind
me to tell you and show you that I love you
without any thought of reward or compensation.

AUGUST 21

*I am the good shepherd. The good shepherd lays
down his life for the sheep.* JOHN 10:11

Dear Lord, as a mom, I feel like a shepherd
sometimes too. Like a shepherd, my sheep
keep me awake at night from time to time. And
my sheep can be quite messy and sometimes
smelly, too. Sometimes my exhausting sheep
run off where they shouldn't be, and I must go
and find them. And in spite of all this, or

maybe because of it, there is nothing I would not do for my sheep. Thank you, Lord, for giving me the perfect example of a Good Shepherd.

AUGUST 22

Wait for the LORD; be strong, and let your heart take courage; wait for the LORD! PSALM 27:14

Waiting is hard, Lord. We are so spoiled with minute microwave menus and instant Internet access that waiting is quickly becoming a lost art. And yet, we are told we must wait for the most important entity of our lives. We must wait for you. Help me today to wait patiently and well for you, Lord. Help me to understand that you, too, are waiting for me.

*We have gifts that differ according to the grace
given to us: prophecy, in proportion to faith.*
ROMANS 12:6

Sometimes, dear God, I look at my children
and marvel at how different each one is from
the other. I see the individuality, special gifts
and graces each one possesses and I am
amazed at how distinct each one is. And then
I think of how you must see each one of your
children—not one of them like another. Help
me to remember that just like you have created
my children to be unique—you have also
created me to be like no one else. Enable me
today to do the one thing you intended for
me—and me alone—to do.

*For where your treasure is, there your heart will be
also.* MATTHEW 6:21

What is my treasure today, Lord? What is it
that you see me valuing and adoring? I would
like to think you see me treasuring my
relationship with you and my family. But I
suspect sometimes you see me cherishing my
house, my car, or even my bank account.

Guide me today, dear Jesus, to begin to let go
of my material treasures so that I am free to
cling more tightly to you.

AUGUST 25

Incline your ear to me; rescue me speedily. Be a
rock of refuge for me, a strong fortress to save me.
PSALM 31:2

What was my rock yesterday, Lord? Was it a
close loved one? Was it my children? Or was I
leaning on my friends for my stability? Help
me today, dear Lord, to embrace the people in
my life as wonderful support systems. But
remind me today that they are not able to
support me as you do. Help me to remember
that the one rock I need to anchor my life
to is you.

August 26

The LORD gave, and the LORD has taken away;
blessed be the name of the LORD. JOB 1:21

Lord, when you give a life to us to love, it is so
easy for us to understand that it is you. That
makes sense to us. But when you take a life
back home to live with you, we often question
you. Forgive us for those doubts. Help us to
understand that there will always be some
things we just won't understand. But regardless
of our ability to comprehend, enable us to
always bless your name.

August 27
Saint Monica

It is not possible that a son of so many tears
should perish. A BISHOP COMFORTING MONICA

Dear God, Saint Monica is the epitome of a
mother who will not give up. She is the poster
mom for perseverance in parenting. Most of us
moms would have given up early on if our
sons had behaved in the fashion of Augustine
in his early years. But she persisted in prayer
and we are all better because of it. Help me,
Lord, to never give up. Give me today, dear

Lord, the perseverance of Saint Monica when it comes to praying for my children.

AUGUST 28
SAINT AUGUSTINE

The world is a book and those who stay at home read only one page. SAINT AUGUSTINE

I suppose St. Augustine wouldn't look too fondly on moms. I suspect Saint Augustine would think mothers who "stay-at-home" (when they aren't running to meetings, school and sporting events, grocery stores, church, volunteer committees, field trips, work, etc.) are only looking at a page in a book with no words and only pictures. But Lord, if the world is a book, thank you for the book you have given to me. It is filled with fingerprints and torn pages and lots of unanswered questions— but it is from you and I love it. Thank you for the Book of Mom you have given to me.

AUGUST 29

....love one another with mutual affection; outdo one another in showing honor. ROMANS 12:10

Lord, wouldn't it be a great world if we were competitive in being compassionate? Wouldn't it be wonderful if we had contests for kindness and matches of mercy? Help me today to instill in my family this desire to outdo each other in the game of goodness. Wouldn't it be wonderful? Wouldn't it be . . . heaven?

AUGUST 30

Gladden the soul of your servant, for to you, O LORD, I lift up my soul. PSALM 86:4

No one really talks much about the soul today, Lord. I mean, you hear of having soul and being a soulmate, but few seem concerned about their soul. Help me today, dear Lord, to concentrate on my soul. Help me to know where it is in me—and where it is going in the future. Allow me to find my soul and lift it up to you.

Rejoice with those who rejoice, weep with those who weep. ROMANS 12:15

Dear Jesus, help me to remember that rejoicing and weeping with each other is what being a family is all about—multiplying each other's joys—dividing the sorrows. Remind me that a family is made up of both the laughter and the tears, but it is the sharing of those ingredients that make a family complete. Sprinkle into our lives, today, the tears we must share to grow. And please, dear Lord, pour into our lives the laughter.

SEPTEMBER 1

For the mountains may depart and the hills be removed, but my steadfast love shall not depart from you, and my covenant of peace shall not be removed, says the LORD, who has compassion on you. ISAIAH 54:10

We get it backwards sometimes, don't we God? We think the world will last forever and the people we love will always be a part of our lives. And yet, we have a tendency to treat you as if you come and go in our lives. But the truth remains, that you are the only constant— the only eternal guarantee in our lives. Your love for us will far outlast the world and the people in it. Help me to embrace this loving truth today, dear God.

SEPTEMBER 2
LABOR DAY*
(1st Monday in September)

Let us therefore no longer pass judgment on one another, but resolve instead never to put a stumbling block or hindrance in the way of another. ROMANS 14:13

I know passing judgment is your job, Lord, not mine. And yet sometimes my heart passes judgment even if I manage to keep it out of my mouth. Please help me with this today, dear Lord. Please remove all judging of others from my heart. Take away any smug feelings of somehow being better. Remind me that you are the final judge, and you are judging me.

SEPTEMBER 3
SAINT GREGORY THE GREAT

So faith by itself, if it has no works, is dead.
JAMES 2:17

Is what I do as a mom considered a work of faith, Lord? When I am up all night with a sick child, or kissing a boo-boo, do you see it as faithful work? Sometimes we moms dream of doing great missionary work one day to help the children of your world. Remind me today, that I am, indeed, doing your work, when I take care of the very children who cry and play and laugh and live in my home.

SEPTEMBER 4

...be filled with the Spirit, as you sing psalms and hymns and spiritual songs among yourselves, singing and making melody to the Lord in your hearts. EPHESIANS 5:18-19

I just can't be in a bad mood when I sing, Lord. There is something about singing that just makes the world a better place. Today, dear Lord, fill my heart with songs of praise and glory to you. Splash harmony throughout my day. Enable me to fill the hearts of others with the same.

SEPTEMBER 5

Let mutual love continue. HEBREWS 13:1

Dear God, mutual love seems pretty easy. It is not hard at all to love those who love us. When someone acts in a loving manner towards us, it is simple for us to treat him or her similarly. But, Lord, it is not easy to love those who treat us in a less-than-loving manner. It is not as natural to love those who don't seem to be loving us at that moment.

Help me today to work on this. Please enable me to love without condition. Help me to love as you love.

SEPTEMBER 6

You also must be patient. Strengthen your hearts, for the coming of the Lord is near. JAMES 5:8

Dear Lord, how do I get a strong heart? I know exercise and diet will help my heart physically to be stronger. But how do I spiritually strengthen my heart? I suspect it is strengthened through loving more, but Lord, the more I love, the more tender my heart seems to become—the more it breaks when others hurt. It's ironic. Or is it?

SEPTEMBER 7
GRANDPARENTS DAY

If then there is any encouragement in Christ, any consolation from love, any sharing in the Spirit, any compassion and sympathy, make my joy complete: be of the same mind, having the same love, being in full accord and of one mind. PHILIPPIANS 2:1-2

Encouragement, sharing, compassion, sympathy, joy. Lord, those are all gifts of good grandparents. What a blessing grandparents are! Thank you for these precious people in our lives who have walked these roads of parenthood before, but are more than happy to travel the road with us again this time. Thank you, Lord! Please bless all the grandparents today with the gifts they give to us every day.

SEPTEMBER 8
BIRTH OF MARY

Give, and it will be given to you. LUKE 6:38

Mary, did you ever want time to yourself? Did you ever feel the need for a day off? How did you do it, Mary? How did you always think of others without feeling resentment? How did you always give without expecting anything in return? Help me today, dear Mother Mary, to understand the incredible gift of giving that you so beautifully understood.

SEPTEMBER 9
SAINT PETER CLAVER

The LORD is my strength and my shield; in him my heart trusts. PSALM 28:7

Some days, Lord, I want a magic shield to put over my children to protect them from the world. I listen to the nightly news and I become fearful to even send them back outside unless I can have some guarantee that they will be protected. Remind me today, dear God, that you are that guarantee. You are that protection. You are our strength and our (magic) shield.

September 10

He who did not withhold his own Son, but gave him up for all of us, will he not with him also give us everything else? Romans 8:32

You have given us everything, dear God. In giving your son to us, you showed us there is no limit to your love. And yet, we so often put imaginary limits on your love, don't we Lord? How many times do we doubt your great love for us in spite of all you have done to prove to us otherwise? Forgive me when I do this. Gently remind me that there may be limits on human love, but there is no limit on your love for humanity.

September 11

The name of the Lord is a strong tower; the righteous run into it and are safe. Proverbs 18:10

Dear Lord, on this day, we recall other towers, which were knocked down by planes being flown into them. We remember the thousands of people who died, and the handful of people (your children also) who were responsible for these tragedies. Lord, while we remember the lives lost on this day, let us pray for the mothers and fathers who were lost, the children who no longer have mothers or fathers, mothers and fathers who lost their children, husbands who no longer have wives, wives who no longer have husbands and all those who today live with the grief and sadness that day brought. We trust in you to help those afflicted. Help us to never forget those affected by 9/11. Let us remember to give respect to you for being there through it all.

SEPTEMBER 12

By this we know that we love the children of God, when we love God and obey his commandments.
1 JOHN 5:2

Dear God, when my children show outward signs of loving each other, not just getting along, but really loving each other, it makes my heart overflow with joy. It's such a simple thing, and yet it is so important. It's one of the best ways they can show me they love me. And so, too, I imagine, it fills you with joy when we, your children, show outward signs of loving each other. Help us to see that this truly is a beautiful circle of love.

September 13
Saint John Chrysostom

*But love your enemies, do good, and lend, expecting
nothing in return. Your reward will be great, and
you will be children of the Most High; for he is kind
to the ungrateful and the wicked.* Luke 6:35

Dear Lord, some days it is hard for my children
to share with each other, even though they
love each other. How can I teach them to share
with the world? How can I teach them to share
with those who may never want to or who
would never be able to share with them? Help
me with this today, dear Jesus. Help me to
teach my children to share. Better yet, guide
me to show them how to share.

September 14
Exaltation of Holy Cross

*Then Jesus told his disciples, "If any want to become
my followers, let them deny themselves and take up
their cross and follow me."* Matthew 16:24

Dear Jesus, ours is a society that seems built
on the theory of "If it feels good, do it!" How
can I instill in my children the concept of
denying themselves and picking up their
crosses in order to follow you? Nobody seeks

suffering, Lord. No one looks for ways to hurt. Help me to raise children who will not be afraid to follow you wherever you might lead them.

SEPTEMBER 15

There they are, bellowing with their mouths, with sharp words on their lips—for "'Who," they think, "will hear us?" PSALM 59:7

I'm afraid I am guilty of occasionally bellowing, dear God. Sometimes I really don't like what comes out of my mouth. And who hears me at these times? My children, and you. Forgive me for the moments of bellowing that I should better control. Help me to swallow words that I shouldn't say, especially those that are so bitter.

SEPTEMBER 16

Honor everyone. Love the family of believers.
1 PETER 2:17

It really does start at home, doesn't it, Lord? It really begins with us. What an amazing responsibility it is to be a mom! To be entrusted to instill these beliefs and this kind of love in our children. What an awesome responsibility it is to raise children and to prepare them for their life—their whole life—not just the life they have here in my home, but for their life outside my home and my care—when they are off at college, or working, or traveling, or caring for a family of their own. What a frightening responsibility it is! Help me teach them to love—so that someday they too will teach others to love.

SEPTEMBER 17

If it is possible, so far as it depends on you, live peaceably with all. ROMANS 12:18

Is it possible, dear Jesus, to live peaceably with all? With everyone? Sometimes I think it is impossible for the people just in my house to live peaceably together. And you are asking us to live peaceably with everyone? What is the secret to this kind of peace, Jesus? Help me today to learn what it takes to live peaceably with all. Enable me to not just learn it, but to live it.

SEPTEMBER 18

The LORD is near to the brokenhearted, and saves the crushed in spirit. PSALM 34:18

LORD, when my children are hurting and their hearts are breaking I feel my own heart swelling with love for them. I have an overwhelming desire and need to make them happy again. How much more, then, do you feel the pain of your children when we are hurting? How much more does your heart break, when we, too, are hurting? Enable me to embrace this truth the next time my heart is breaking. Help me to run straight to you with my broken heart.

SEPTEMBER 19

And if I go and prepare a place for you, I will come again and will take you to myself, so that where I am, there you may be also. JOHN 14:3

Everywhere I go, Lord, my children want to come too. Sometimes, I want to take them with me, but I just can't. And so I promise them that they will go with me one day. Was that the way it was with you when you had to leave? Did you want to take everyone with you then, but you knew it wasn't time yet? How comforting it is to think of you waiting for us, wanting so dearly to take us where you have gone. Waiting patiently for the day when it will be our turn to go with you.

SEPTEMBER 20

Whoever says, "I am in the light," while hating a brother or sister, is still in the darkness. 1 JOHN 2:9

It must make you so sad, Lord, to see hatred among your children. I won't even allow my children to use the word. I know I might be able to keep it out of their vocabularies, but I am afraid I won't be able to keep it out of their lives forever. Help me encourage my children by example to walk in the light of love rather than creep in the shadows of darkness.

SEPTEMBER 21
SAINT MATTHEW THE EVANGELIST

His master said to him, "Well done, good and trustworthy slave; you have been trustworthy in a few things, I will put you in charge of many things; enter into the joy of your master." MATTHEW 25:21

Sometimes, Lord, I wonder if you are testing me with my children. Are you seeing how I react to a temper tantrum before you put me in charge of a bigger crisis? Are you waiting to see how I handle a quarrel between siblings before you see what I can do for world peace? Mother Teresa once said, "We can do no great things, only small things with great love." Is that what you are testing me on, Lord? And if so, how am I doing?

SEPTEMBER 22

*Lead me in your truth, and teach me, for you are
the God of my salvation; for you I wait all day long.*
PSALM 25:5

It's easy for us as parents to forget we need
parenting, God. It is easy to get wrapped up in
the false notion that we already know what we
need to know. But the truth is we are coaches
who need coaching. We are teachers who need
teaching. We are children who need our Father.
Dear God, we are sinners, and we need you.

SEPTEMBER 23

*God looks down from heaven on humankind to see
if there are any who are wise, who seek after God.*
PSALM 53:2

It's a good thing you have perfect vision, Lord.
Because I can only imagine that some days it is
hard to see the good people on earth due to
the fact that evil draws so much attention to
itself. Help me today to have your perfect
vision in seeing the goodness over the evil.
Enable me today, dear Lord, to have my
Father's eyes.

*See that none of you repays evil for evil, but always
seek to do good to one another and to all.*
1 THESSALONIANS 5:15

You don't want us seeking revenge, do you
Lord? It's just that it is easier for us to imagine
repaying evil with evil rather than turning the
other cheek? Help me today, dear Lord, to seek
to do good to others even when someone does
something to me that is less than good. Please
strengthen my heart so that I might, indeed,
turn the other cheek. And please, dear Lord,
strengthen my cheek.

SEPTEMBER 25

Think of us in this way, as servants of Christ.
1 CORINTHIANS 4:1-2

Dear Lord, sometimes we moms suffer from low self-esteem. There is rarely anything we can point to at the end of the day and say, "Look. I did that." We do laundry, which never ends. We feed kids, who never stop eating. We bath little ones, who always get dirty again. Help me today, dear Lord, when my self-esteem starts to fade due to one more seemingly endless menial job. Help me to look at the preciousness of the big picture of parenting. Enable me to take a deep breath and say, "Look, I am a servant of Christ."

SEPTEMBER 26

It is well with those who deal generously and lend, who conduct their affairs with justice. PSALM 112:5

We worry a lot about justice, Lord. Millions of hours and dollars are spent discussing what laws we truly need to have in order to live well. Help us today, dear Lord, to remember that you already gave us the laws we need to live well when you gave us the Ten

Commandments. Help us to focus our energy
on learning and living those laws.

SEPTEMBER 27

I will let you find me, says the LORD. JEREMIAH 29:14

Dear God, I love the idea that you will let us
find you. I know when I play hide-and-seek
with my little ones they get frustrated if they
truly can't find me after even a short while.
And so I let them find me. They then feel a
sense of accomplishment. This must be how it
is with you. You always know where we are.
You always know you can be found. You let us
find you when we need you the most.

SEPTEMBER 28

Ascribe to the LORD the glory of his name;
worship the LORD in holy splendor. PSALM 29:2

Today, dear Lord, I woke up in a warm bed.
Thank you for that. I made breakfast for my
children. Thank you for that. I met their needs
as they arose throughout the day just as you
met my needs. Thank you for that. I will
return again, eventually, to that warm bed once
more to begin it all over again. Thank you for
that, and so much more.

SEPTEMBER 29
SAINT MICHAEL, GABRIEL AND RAPHAEL,
ARCHANGELS

For it is written, "He will command his angels concerning you, to protect you." LUKE 4:10

Thank you, God, for your messengers that you send to us. Thank you for your angels that show us your mercy, power and judgment. Help me to remember that you are with me in many ways. Make it part of my mission today, dear Lord, to seek the angels that you have sent just for me.

SEPTEMBER 30
SAINT JEROME

Let those who are wise give heed to these things, and consider the steadfast love of the LORD. PSALM 107:43

Dear Lord, I want to be wise. I want to learn what it is you want me to learn, but sometimes I am afraid of what the lesson has in store for me. Help me, today, to embrace all the lessons of my life that you are teaching me. Give to me the strength to learn and live your will for me.

OCTOBER 1
SAINT THERESE OF LISIEUX

It is such a folly to pass one's time fretting, instead of resting quietly on the heart of Jesus.
SAINT THERESE OF LISIEUX

Dear Lord, help me today to learn from the wonderful example of your passionate servant, Saint Therese, how becoming more like a child will bring me closer to you. Help me to see that just as my children run to me when they are afraid, that I too need to run to you. Enable me to not waste precious time with needless worry, when I could, instead, be resting quietly in your arms.

OCTOBER 2
GUARDIAN ANGELS

Do not neglect to show hospitality to strangers, for by doing that some have entertained angels without knowing it. HEBREWS 13:2

Have you ever sent me an angel, Lord, to test me? And if you did, did I pass the test? Did I feed the hungry, satiate the thirsty, or cheer the sad? Or did I, instead, walk away, not noticing what I should have seen? Help me today, Lord, to act in a way that will help me pass these tests that just might be my test of a lifetime.

OCTOBER 3

Humble yourselves before the Lord, and he will exalt you. JAMES 4:10

Dear God, I used to think that nothing humbled me more than to stand beside one of your majestic oceans marveling at your power. But then, you placed each of my babies in my arms and I soon learned what it truly means to be humbled. When I think of the precious gifts you have given me, dear Lord, I know I am not worthy of love that great. But thank you for believing I am.

OCTOBER 4
SAINT FRANCIS OF ASISSI

Preach the gospel everywhere you go. When necessary, use words. SAINT FRANCIS OF ASSISI

Dear God, I have always heard the phrase, "Actions speak louder than words," but I may not always act like I have heard it. Forgive me, Lord for the times when my actions contradict the beliefs I speak of so often. Enable me today to be more like your peace-loving servant, Saint Francis, and preach the Gospel everywhere I go, whether or not I even speak at all.

OCTOBER 5

But you are a chosen race . . . God's own people, in order that you may proclaim the mighty acts of him who called you out of darkness into his marvelous light. 1 PETER 2:9

I love to think of being a mom as being a member of a chosen race, your own people, God. I love to feel that this vocation of motherhood was handed to me as part of your higher plan for my purpose. Please remind me of that, Lord, when I get caught up in the cooking and the cleaning, the wiping and the whining. Remind me that it might be chaos, but it's also my calling.

OCTOBER 6

Show yourself in all respects a model of good works, and in your teaching show integrity. TITUS 2:7

There is a lot of responsibility that comes with being a mom, dear Lord. Every time we bring home a new child, I suspect we also need to bring home a better attitude and a better spirituality than we had before. I want so badly to be a perfect role model for my kids, but I cannot be perfect. But you, dear Jesus, are perfect. Help me to watch you more closely so that I will be a better role model for those who are so closely watching me.

OCTOBER 7
OUR LADY OF THE ROSARY

I have taught you the way of wisdom; I have led you in the paths of uprightness. PROVERBS 4:11

Dear Mother Mary, you do teach the way of wisdom by being so wise. You teach the path to patience by being so patient with us. You lead us to righteousness by pointing the way to your son, Jesus Christ. I want to do this for my children, too. Dear Blessed Mother, I want to be like you, when I grow up.

OCTOBER 8

Holy, holy, holy, the Lord God the Almighty, who was and is and is to come. REVELATION 4:8

Dear Lord, you were here on earth teaching, preaching and dying for my sins. You are with us now, by loving us and coming to us through the Eucharist. You will come again one day in glory to take us home. Thank you, Lord. You are my past, my present and my future.

OCTOBER 9

When you walk, your step will not be hampered; and if you run, you will not stumble. PROVERBS 4:12

Dear Lord, when my children were first learning to walk, they fell a lot. I would offer my hand to steady them, but still they insisted on trying to walk on their own, in spite of the bumps and bruises that would inevitably follow. I'm like that, Lord. When I insist on doing things on my own, I stumble and get hurt. But my step is so much more steady when I take your hand and allow you to lead me.

October 10

For thus said the LORD God, the Holy One of Israel:
In returning and rest you shall be saved; in
quietness and in trust shall be your strength.
ISAIAH 30:15

Lord, if my strength has to do with quietness,
I'm in trouble. You know that this is the noisy
time of my life. The daily sounds that fill my
home range from laughter to tears and from
screaming to sighs. And then there is the
music, the Internet and the television. And I'm
supposed to rest and be quiet? I suspect there
will be quiet in these noisy halls one day, Lord.
But until then, help me to rejoice in the noise
and find my strength in you. And if possible,
help me to find some earplugs.

October 11

The gifts and the calling of God are irrevocable.
ROMANS 11:29

What awesome gifts you have given me, dear
God! When I wake up in the morning and
hear the sound of my human alarm clock, also
known as my little one, I want to say: "Thank
you, Lord!" When I am running on two good
legs to stop a toddler from doing something

that a toddler shouldn't do, please let me say,
"Thank you, Lord!" When I am exhausted
from a day of tending to my blessings, I will
say, "Thank you, Lord" for the chance to be
this tired and for the chance to have these
blessings.

OCTOBER 12

*And now, my children, listen to me: happy are those
who keep my ways.* PROVERBS 8:32

How many times, dear Lord, do I end up
telling my children, "I told you so?" How
many times would something undesirable have
been avoided if only they had listened to me?
How infinitely more times have I failed to
listen to you, Lord? Forgive me for those
times. Please help me today to listen to you as
I want to be listened to by my children.

OCTOBER 13
COLUMBUS DAY*
(Second Monday in October)

*Steadfast love and faithfulness will meet;
righteousness and peace will kiss each other.*
PSALM 85:10

It seems so obvious, Lord, that what a child
learns in his home he carries with him into the
world. And yet sometimes, we fail to remember
this vital component of a person's personality.
Help me, please, to blanket my children in an
atmosphere of love, faithfulness, righteousness
and peace so that they will be better buffered
to face what the world throws at them.

OCTOBER 14

*Yet, O LORD, you are our Father; we are the clay,
and you are our potter; we are all the work of your
hand.* ISAIAH 64:8

Dear God, was it fun to create the world and
everyone in it? So many times I have watched
my children playing with colored clay, creating
worlds of blue trees and green cats. What fun
they have creating something brand new! How
awesome it is that you created life from
nothing at all. Thank you, Lord, for creating

life. Thank you for your masterpieces that are
unique and precious and don't end up stuck in
my carpet.

OCTOBER 15
SAINT TERESA OF AVILA

*Settle yourself in solitude and you will come upon
God in yourself.* SAINT TERESA OF AVILA

Lord, you know my days are full, but they sure
aren't full of a lot of solitude. Some days, I
don't think I can find the time to find me in
myself—let alone find you in there. But thank
you, Lord, for always being with me even
when I am too busy to find you.

OCTOBER 16

*Do not, therefore, abandon that confidence of yours;
it brings a great reward.* HEBREWS 10:35

Dear Jesus, some days I feel very confident. I
think I have it all figured out. Some days I feel
that I know how to be a mom and am doing it
well. But then someone seemingly changes the
rules of this game and I am back to knowing
very little once again. When this happens, dear
Lord, help me to see that my confidence
belongs in you, and not in me. And as long as I
can remember that, the rules of this game of
life will never change.

OCTOBER 17

*You shall put these words of mine in your heart and
soul, and you shall bind them as a sign on your
hand, and fix them as an emblem on your forehead.*
DEUTERONOMY 11:18

Dear Lord, why is it that I continually search
for books on how to live my life well? I am
always interested in reading how I can be
better, do better and live better. Why is it that I
so often forget that I already own the best book
that tells me how to be, do and live? Help me

to pick up my Bible more often, dear Lord. Not only to read it, but also to live it.

OCTOBER 18
SAINT LUKE, EVANGELIST

Just so, I tell you, there is joy in the presence of the angels of God over one sinner who repents.
LUKE 15:10

I know what you mean on this one, Jesus. It is true, we moms love the child who consistently chooses the right path and does the right thing. How blest they are! But there is a special joy, a special love for the child who has stumbled in the past and who now chooses what is right and tries so hard to walk the path of goodness. Thank you for these moments of joy, dear Lord. They give us such hope and confirm our own salvation.

OCTOBER 19

Teach [my words] to your children, talking about them when you are at home and when you are away, when you lie down and when you rise.
DEUTERONOMY 11:19

Dear Lord, my kids are saturated with other people's words running through their minds and lives. Teachers, coaches, movie stars, singers, all have an impact on my children for better or for worse. Help me to balance the words of others with your Word, dear Lord. Today, please help me to work your Word more and more into my conversations with my children. Enable me to make your way as natural for them as breathing.

OCTOBER 20

The way of the righteous is level; O Just One, you make smooth the path of the righteous. ISAIAH 26:7

Every now and then, dear Lord, I feel as if I am driving down this road of life and all is passing along quite well. But then, I hit a rough spot, a bump in the road, a detour. Help me not to panic if my road gets tricky today, Lord. Please enable me to turn to you so that you can point

me in the right direction. And help me also to
realize that you have already paved the way
for me.

OCTOBER 21

*The LORD is gracious and merciful, slow to anger
and abounding in steadfast love.* PSALM 145:8

Some days, dear God, I fall short on being slow
to anger and abounding in steadfast love. I
want to be more patient. Please help me with
this. When things start to go wrong today,
when we are running late, when something
spills or breaks or just doesn't go according to
my plan, help me to breathe deeply. And when
I do, please help me to feel your breath of
gracious and merciful love washing over me.

OCTOBER 22

For the promise is for you, for your children, and for all who are far away, everyone whom the Lord our God calls to him. ACTS 2:39

When my little one asks me to do something for him, Lord, he always ends with, "You promise?" And when I say, "Yes," he rests assured, believing that my word is as good as gold. That's the way I see your promise, dear Lord. The promise you have made for me, for my children and for us all. Thank you for your promise! It is, indeed, better than *gold*.

OCTOBER 23

But God proves his love for us in that while we still were sinners Christ died for us. ROMANS 5:8

When I was little, dear Jesus, I used to believe that I would be punished for my sins. But now that I have a better understanding of your great love for me and how my sins keep me away from you in spite of the incredible price you already paid for me, I have come to understand something else. I am not so much punished *for* my sins, as I am punished *by* my sins.

Help me today, dear Lord Jesus, to stop
allowing my sins to keep me away from you.

OCTOBER 24

*May the God of hope fill you with all joy and peace
in believing, so that you may abound in hope by the
power of the Holy Spirit.* ROMANS 15:13

Dear God, I want to be filled with all joy and
peace in believing. I want to be a fountain of
hope with nothing but positive thoughts
spewing forth. But sometimes what spews forth
from me is nothing I want to be covered in.
Cleanse me today of all negativity. Enable me
to embrace the full message of believing in you
so that I can be filled with overflowing joy and
peace.

OCTOBER 25

*O LORD, you will ordain peace for us, for indeed,
all that we have done, you have done for us.*
ISAIAH 26:12

Dear Lord, please help me the next time I feel
overwhelmed (and you and I both know there
will be a next time). Aid me when I start
mentally counting off the list of chores and
duties that I must do in the course of my day.
Help me to see them as bountiful blessings
instead of tedious tasks. Enable me to
understand that all I have done is simply done
by your grace. All I have done, you have done
for me.

OCTOBER 26

*O LORD of hosts, happy is everyone who trusts in
you.* PSALM 84:12

When I truly trust in you, dear Lord, I am
indeed happy. But when I try to take control of
my life, when I try to write the chapters of the
novel that is my life, I then start to fear. It is
then that I start to focus on my limitations, my
frailties and my weaknesses. Remind me over
and over again, dear Lord, that you are writing

this novel of my life, not me. And there is no good reason for me not to trust in you for how the book turns out.

OCTOBER 27

Hallelujah! Salvation and glory and power to our God, for his judgments are true and just.
REVELATION 19:1-2

Hallelujah! What a great word that is, God! Hallelujah! Nothing else quite sums up the feeling of joy for what you have done for us. No other word can speak for what you have given us. No other word does justice to the explosion of joy in my heart when I think of you loving me, dear Lord. Hallelujah!

OCTOBER 28
SAINTS SIMON AND JUDE, APOSTLES

In your steadfast love you led the people whom you redeemed; you guided them by your strength to your holy abode. EXODUS 15:13

Love, love, love. Lord, you tell us over and over again what it is all about. It is about love. And yet we make it so difficult. We spend so much precious time wondering what it is all about, wondering what the answer is. And you patiently tell us. It is about love. Help me today to remember your love. Help me today to live your love. Help me today to give love wherever I go and in all that I do.

OCTOBER 29

. . . this is the true grace of God. Stand fast in it. 1 PETER 5:12

I want to stand in your grace, Dear God. I want to stand fast in your grace. But I confess, I had to look up what "grace" truly meant. My dictionary tells me it is holiness, kindness, mercy and love. My heart tells me it is all I need. Thank you for your amazing grace, dear Lord. Help me to stand in it today.

OCTOBER 30

. . . endurance produces character, and character produces hope. ROMANS 5:4

We don't hear a lot about character these days, do we, Lord? It has somehow gotten overlooked among the desired qualities of wealth, beauty and popularity. And yet, you constantly remind us that it is not about our bodies or our bank accounts. Rather, what matters is who we are and the content of our character. Help me today to endure what I must endure to produce character. Help me to produce hope.

OCTOBER 31

But I call upon God, and the LORD will save me.
Evening and morning and at noon, I utter my
complaint and moan, and he will hear my voice.
PSALM 55:16-17

Some days, dear Lord, I confess that I get tired
of hearing all the complaints and moans that
echo throughout my house when I ask for
something to be done. How do you do it,
Lord? How do you listen to millions of us
whining and bemoaning what you have asked
us to do? Forgive me for this. And thank you,
Father, for not giving up on this child in the
evening, morning or noon.

NOVEMBER 1
ALL SAINTS

Are any among you suffering? They should pray.
Are any cheerful? They should sing songs of praise.
JAMES 5:13

Dear Lord, the saints have taught us the value
of praying when suffering. As a matter of fact,
the saints teach us the value of praying for
suffering. Forgive me if I can't do that just yet.
But Lord, just as it is second nature for me to
pray when I am suffering or have a problem, I
want it to be second nature to praise you when
I am happy. Enable me today to turn to you
when my heart is glad. Remind me to thank
you for everything, even suffering.

NOVEMBER 2
ALL SOULS

Even though I walk through the darkest valley, I
fear no evil; for you are with me. PSALM 23:4

You are with me, Lord. You are with me. What
comfort that gives me! How many times do I
reassure my children by telling them "Don't
worry—I'm right here." Help me today, dear
Lord, to turn to you in my times of trouble.
Enable me to feel you with me, telling me,
"Don't worry. I'm right here."

NOVEMBER 3
SAINT MARTIN DE PORRES

Those who despise their neighbors are sinners,
but happy are those who are kind to the poor.
PROVERBS 14:21

Dear God, help me today to learn from the life
of your faithful servant, Saint Martin de Porres,
how to treat everyone lovingly, regardless of
how they look, how rich or poor they are, or
how they treat me. Even though I don't think I
have any prejudice in my mind, please remove
from my heart any hidden bigotry or hatred
that might be lurking there. Enable me to
understand that we all truly are brothers and
sisters in Christ. Help me to teach my children
that today.

NOVEMBER 4

He must manage his own household well, keeping
his children submissive and respectful in every
way—for if someone does not know how to manage
his own household, how can he take care of God's
church? 1 TIMOTHY 3:4-5

Some days, dear Lord, I don't feel like I am
managing anything. Crying kids, overflowing
laundry, work deadlines, obstacle courses of

toys and books in every room of my house, make me feel as if I don't even know where to begin. Help me to learn to do a better job with managing the little things in my life so that I might one day be able to manage the big things.

NOVEMBER 5

Be angry but do not sin; do not let the sun go down on your anger. EPHESIANS 4:26

We are not always going to agree on everything, are we, Lord? With so many opinions and personalities living under one roof, we are bound to butt heads from time to time. Help us when this happens to be fair and loving with each other even in our disagreements. Please enable us, Lord, to remember we love the person, even if we dislike the opinion.

NOVEMBER 6

But I will hope continually, and will praise you yet more and more. PSALM 71:14

Hope is a wonderful word, Lord. It is faith, trust, belief and assurance all rolled into one word. It is what I hold onto when things are not going the way I had planned. It is the silver lining of a cloud. It is my glass being half-full. Help me today to have hope during darker hours to come. Help me today to have hope in you, always.

NOVEMBER 7

Discipline your children, and they will give you rest; they will give delight to your heart. PROVERBS 29:17

Disciplining is hard, Lord. Especially when we are busy. We all have busy schedules—work outside the home, work inside the home, soccer practice, ballet rehearsals, PTA meetings, outings with friends, co-workers, relatives, etc. With all that we have to do in any given week, it comes as no surprise that we often don't have enough time to simply be with our children. And what time we do get to spend with them, we hesitate to spend disciplining. Help us to see that sometimes the most loving thing we can do for our children is discipline them. Help us to raise children who will learn to appreciate the value of consequences.

It is better to live in a desert land than with a contentious and fretful wife. PROVERBS 21:19

Oops. I think I need help with this, Lord. I know that sometimes I am a less than pleasant wife, friend, mother or co-worker. Sometimes I am downright contentious and fretful. It is so easy to see what is wrong with others. But it is so much harder to turn those same critical eyes back on ourselves. Help me today, dear Lord to see myself more clearly. Help me to be a better person. Allow me today to concentrate on changing what is wrong with me instead of always trying to change those around me.

NOVEMBER 9

*Even children make themselves known by their
acts, by whether what they do is pure and right.*
PROVERBS 20:11

Dear God, so much of our children's future is
riding on the decisions they make today. I
realize I cannot be involved in every decision
they will make from this point on. But you can
be in those thoughts, actions and deeds that
are to come, Lord. I pray today that you will
always be present in the decisions my children
will make in their lives. Guide them. Direct
them. Please protect them from themselves,
when necessary.

NOVEMBER 10
SAINT LEO THE GREAT

*He will feed his flock like a shepherd; he will gather
the lambs in his arms, and carry them in his bosom,
and gently lead the mother sheep.* ISAIAH 40:11

Today I pray, dear Lord, that you will, indeed,
gently guide this mother sheep. Guide me to
go the right places, do the right thing, set the
right example. Help me to understand that my
little lambs will, indeed, follow me. Better yet,
Lord, please help me to step out of the way
enough so that they will learn to follow you,
their shepherd.

NOVEMBER 11
VETERANS DAY

He will wipe every tear from their eyes. Death will be no more. REVELATION 21:4

Dear God, a mother spends a lot of her time wiping tears away. It is such a sign of comfort. It is such an act of healing. I love the image of you wiping away our tears when we hurt. I love the idea of you doing that for us. Help me today to embrace that idea as a reality. Help me to always run to you to wipe away my tears.

NOVEMBER 12

Fathers, do not provoke your children, or they may lose heart. COLOSSIANS 3:21

On occasion, dear Lord, I have witnessed parents in a public place lose their patience with their child. I recognize the signs and am sometimes at a loss as to what I can do to help. Please guide me in these moments, Lord. Help me to know when to step in and when to stay out. Help me not to judge, but to help. And enable me to keep my own patience with my own children and all of yours as well.

NOVEMBER 13

Take my yoke upon you, and learn from me; for I am gentle and humble in heart, and you will find rest for your souls. MATTHEW 11:29

You are always thinking of us, dear Lord. You are always thinking of us. You gently guide us and teach us. You don't want us to suffer, and yet you know there are some things we simply must go through in order to get to where we are going. Thank you for being there for me, Lord. Thank you for walking beside me and helping me to bear my burdens.

NOVEMBER 14

All shall give as they are able, according to the blessing of the LORD your God that he has given you. DEUTERONOMY 16:17

Dear God, when I think of all the blessings you have given me, I know that I will never be able to repay you. I know I cannot out-give you. But help me today, dear Lord, to live my life in a way that truly tries to say, "Thank you." Enable me today to give back to you by giving to others more and more. Help me to give, not just until it hurts, but until it *helps*.

So we have known and believe the love that God has for us. God is love, and those who abide in love abide in God, and God abides in them. 1 JOHN 4:16

I want to abide in love, Lord. I want love to bounce from wall to wall in my home. I want to always be able to find the thread of love that is woven throughout the squabbles. I want to notice the shadow of love that looms over the disagreements. I want to always be able to discover the presence of love in the personality conflicts in my home. Help us, dear Lord, to see love in everything. Help us, dear Lord, to see you in everything.

NOVEMBER 16

Let another praise you, and not your own mouth—
a stranger, and not your own lips. PROVERBS 27:2

Dear God, my dad used to joke, "If you don't
toot your own horn, it won't get tooted." We
are all a society of people who want a pat on
the back. We want praise, compliments and
applause. But we moms don't get a lot of
applause for the laundry, the cooking, the
taming of temper tantrums, or even the
working outside of the home. Help me today
to focus on my vocation and not adulation. But
maybe, just maybe, you could send me
someone today to toot my horn.

NOVEMBER 17

Be careful to obey all these words that I command
you today, so that it may go well with you and with
your children after you forever, because you will be
doing what is good and right in the sight of the
LORD your God. DEUTERONOMY 12:28

Dear Lord, it is easy to forget that what I do
and don't do today will greatly affect my
children. It is easy to forget that when I don't
live my life the way you have commanded, I
am not only hurting myself, but I am also

hurting my children. Help me today, dear Lord, to live my life as a life of good faith. Help me, please, to follow your words as if my children's lives depended on it.

NOVEMBER 18

Brothers and sisters, do not be weary in doing what is right. 2 THESSALONIANS 3:13

Dear God, it is hard to get everyone to church every week. It is hard to enforce your words all the time. It is hard to remind my children to be kind, to think of others and to pray. It is hard to follow through on consequences when my children break a rule. Help me to remember today, dear Father, that it all may be hard, but it is, indeed, right.

NOVEMBER 19

*To get wisdom is to love oneself; to keep
understanding is to prosper.* PROVERBS 19:8

Lord, there is so much I don't know. There is
so much I don't understand. I don't understand
why children have to suffer. I don't understand
how someone with so much to live for could
die. I don't understand why you give us some
people only to take them away. Help me with
this today, dear Lord, to understand when I
truly need to understand. And for all the other
times, please gently remind me that you have
called me not to understand, but to trust.

NOVEMBER 20

*O give thanks to the LORD, for he is good, for his
steadfast love endures forever.* PSALM 136:1

So much comes and goes into and out of our
lives, dear Lord. We have become a disposable
society. We have become a nation that accepts
that the only thing constant is change. But the
truth is, the only thing constant is you and
your love for us. Thank you, Lord for your
love. Thank you for showing me what forever
means.

NOVEMBER 21
PRESENTATION OF MARY

The mother was especially admirable and worthy of honorable memory. 2 MACCABEES 7:20

Dear Mother Mary, our days are full of sound bites and news flashes about how we should act and be and live. Bigger is better. More is even better yet. But you are there to remind us that very few things are important. You remind us that it is important to live admirably and serve the Lord. You remind us that it is not who we are, but what we are that is important. It's not about what we have in our homes. It's about what we have in our hearts. Thank you, Mother Mary, for living this lesson so well.

NOVEMBER 22

Comfort, O comfort my people, says your God.
ISAIAH 40:1

Thank you, Lord, for giving me arms to hold
my children when they are hurting. Thank you
for blessing me with hands to reach out and
dry their tears. Thank you for giving me the
right words when they need to hear them.
Thank you for the ears and the heart you gave
me to listen with when words aren't enough.
Thank you for the blessing of being able to
comfort your people, O Lord.

NOVEMBER 23
CHRIST THE KING

*...nor height, nor depth, nor anything else in all
creation, will be able to separate us from the love of
God in Christ Jesus our Lord.* ROMANS 8:39

My dear Lord, there is nowhere my children
can go where I would not love them. There is
nothing they could do that would stop me
from being their mom. How much more
awesome, then, is your love for us? How much
more incredible is the fact that there is not a
place on Earth or in Heaven that you would

not love us? Thank you for this love! It moves us as well as moves with us.

NOVEMBER 24

Listen to advice and accept instruction, that you may gain wisdom for the future. PROVERBS 19:20

I know I need advice and I know I need instruction, but whom do I listen to, dear Lord? There is a book, a lecturer, a specialist, or an expert available today who would be willing to give me advice on anything I might need to ask. Help me with this today, dear God. Grant me the grace of discernment in knowing when the advice that is coming my way is something I need to hold onto, or when it is simply something I need to let go. Remind me to seek your advice at all times.

NOVEMBER 25

A word fitly spoken is like apples of gold in a setting of silver. PROVERBS 25:11

Dear God, you know my words are sometimes more like bitter apples than golden ones. Forgive me for this, please. Forgive me for the times I have spoken out of pride or anger. Forgive me for the times my words have hurt instead of healed. Help me today to speak the way I would like to be spoken to. Please take away any bitterness in my words, as well as in my heart.

NOVEMBER 26

In my Father's house there are many dwelling places. If it were not so, would I have told you that I go to prepare a place for you? JOHN 14:2

You are preparing a place for me, dear Jesus. Thank you! No one prepares a place for a mom here on earth. We are the ones who prepare all the places for others. We are the ones who have to get ready for all the trips and journeys. So, thank you, even more, for preparing a place for me in heaven, dear Lord. Help me today to live my life in a way that, indeed, prepares me for that trip of a lifetime.

NOVEMBER 27

And forgive us our debts, as we also have forgiven our debtors. MATTHEW 6:12

What a beautiful way you taught us to pray, dear Jesus! It's so beautiful, but do I do this? Do I forgive others the way I want to be forgiven? When someone apologizes to me, am I capable of truly forgiving and letting it go? Help me today, dear Lord Jesus, to let go of any bitterness or resentment I might be holding onto in my heart. Help me to forgive others the way I want to be forgiven.

NOVEMBER 28
THANKSGIVING*

[I am] singing aloud a song of thanksgiving, and telling all your wondrous deeds. PSALM 26:7

Lord, if I truly tried to sing a song of all the wondrous deeds you have done for me, it would take a lot longer than the one day that we call Thanksgiving Day. It would take longer than the three hundred and sixty-four other days in a year as well. I suspect, dear Lord, that I could sing songs of praise to you from today until the day my song is silenced on this earth and it would not be enough to praise you rightly or thank you for all you have given me. But I want to try, dear Lord. Please accept my song of thanksgiving today.

NOVEMBER 29

When the cares of my heart are many, your consolations cheer my soul. PSALM 94:19

Today, dear Jesus, I want to pray for those who are hurting in this world. I pray you will be with them where they need it the most. Whether it is a physical body ache or an emotional heartbreak, please be with those

today who feel there is no one there for them.
What is more, please help me today, dear Lord,
to do what I should do to help them as well.

NOVEMBER 30

*See, I have set before you today life and prosperity,
death and adversity.* DEUTERONOMY 30:15

Dear God, we say we want it all, but that's not
true, is it? We really don't want any of the bad
stuff. We want life and prosperity, but not
death and adversity. We want the rainbow, but
not the rain. Help me with this today, dear
Lord. Enable me to accept whatever you have
set before me. Help me be able to thank you
for it all.

DECEMBER 1
ADVENT BEGINS*

I consider that the sufferings of this present time are not worth comparing with the glory about to be revealed to us. ROMANS 8:18

What a wonderful thought, dear Lord! No suffering that we will endure, no pain that we must face, will even begin to compare in magnitude to the glory that you have planned for us. What a beautiful promise! What incredible encouragement! Help me dear Lord, to hold onto that thought the next time adversity comes knocking at my door. Help me to remember that you are patiently waiting behind another door with glory that I cannot imagine. And please give me the strength to open both doors.

DECEMBER 2

Make no friends with those given to anger, and do not associate with hotheads. PROVERBS 22:24

Lord, I confess, I want to be able to pick my children's friends forever. I want to be the one who always says yes or no to a particular play-date, or real teenage-date. But I know unless I am planning on never letting my children leave

the house, they will be meeting others I might
not know, or even approve of. Guard my
children, Lord. Please help them to make good
decisions in their friendships. And help me to
know when it really is a better idea for me to
insist they simply stay home instead.

DECEMBER 3

*Like good stewards of the manifold grace of God,
serve one another with whatever gift each of you
has received.* 1 PETER 4:10

Dear God, what gift have you given me that
you want me to share with others? Have I used
it yet, or am I unintentionally saving it for
another day? Help me today, dear Lord to
begin to live in a way that uses all the gifts you
intended for me to use. Make it impossible for
me to hold back on these gifts with others.
Please remind me that no one benefits from an
unopened gift.

For it is the nations of the world that strive after all these things, and your Father knows that you need them. Instead, strive for his kingdom, and these things will be given to you as well. LUKE 12:30-31

We want our children to have it all, Lord. And so we strive towards signing them up for every sport, class and musical lesson ever known to man. We want them to have it all. Help me today, though, to strive towards focusing less and less on the things the world teaches and begin helping my children focus more and more on the things you teach. Enable me, Lord, to make you a part of their lives like nothing else. Help me to understand that only then will my children have it all.

DECEMBER 5

Do not boast about tomorrow, for you do not know what a day may bring. PROVERBS 27:1

Lord, who knows what tomorrow will bring? We tend to pretend that tomorrow will be just like today, and on and on it will go. But it doesn't always work that way, does it? Help me to live today not in fear of tomorrow, but never taking it for granted. Enable me, Lord, to find peace in the knowledge that you do, indeed, know what tomorrow will bring.

DECEMBER 6

Better is a dry morsel with quiet than a house full of feasting with strife. PROVERBS 17:1

Lord, you know my house is rarely quiet. There is usually some sort of sound echoing throughout the halls. It might be either the sound of intoxicating laughter, dejected tears, joyful singing or angry arguments bouncing around. And some days all those sounds might be heard at the same time in my house. But, Lord, help me at each of those deafening times to be able to still hear you in my heart and in my home.

DECEMBER 7

You are my hiding place and my shield; I hope in your word. PSALM 119:114

I confess, Lord, some days I want to hide. Some days I want to hide from my kids, from my husband, from my family members or from my friends. Some days I want to hide from the obligations of my world. Now, I know that is not very responsible of me and not very grown-up of me. But Lord, some days I just want to hide. On those days, please remind me that you are my hiding place. With you I will always find what I seek. Thank you for being my shelter. I know you will nudge me when it is time for me to come out of hiding.

DECEMBER 8
IMMACULATE CONCEPTION

Now faith is the assurance of things hoped for, the conviction of things not seen. HEBREWS 11:1

Dear Mother Mary, what did your parents think about all that was asked of you? From the very beginning of your life, they knew you were special. And yet, you were still their baby girl. How hard it must have been for them to comprehend the role in salvation you were

called to play. What faith they had to have!
Help me please, Mother Mary, to have that
same faith that joyfully trusts in God's plan,
even when there may be no understanding.

DECEMBER 9

*. . . for God did not give us a spirit of cowardice, but
rather a spirit of power and of love and of self-
discipline.* 2 TIMOTHY 1:7

So many times, dear Lord, I find myself telling
my children not to be afraid of something. I try
to help them overcome their fears. Please guide
my words at these tender times. Help me to
instill in them a spirit of empowerment so that
they will not go through life fearful. Help me
to help them develop a sense of self-discipline
so that they will not put themselves into
situations of danger. Remind me to remind
them that you are always with them. And
please, dear Lord, help me listen to these
words as well.

DECEMBER 10

A friend loves at all times, and kinsfolk are born to share adversity. PROVERBS 17:17

Today, dear God, I want to pray for those who are alone in this world. I pray for those who find themselves without a family. I have never known how people face adversity in their lives alone—without a family and without you. Help me today to reach out to someone who might be alone, for whatever reason. Allow me to remind them that they are a part of your family, Lord.

DECEMBER 11

For the wages of sin is death, but the free gift of God is eternal life in Christ Jesus our Lord. ROMANS 6:23

Dear God, we are so accepting of the fact that nothing in life is free, especially around Christmas time. But that's not true when it comes to you, is it? You have selflessly and freely given us your son, Jesus Christ. And in this incredible gift lies the free gift of eternal life. What an awesome gift, Lord, during this Christmas season and always.

DECEMBER 12
OUR LADY OF GUADALUPE

The angel said to her, "The Holy Spirit will come upon you, and the power of the Most High will overshadow you; therefore the child to be born will be holy; he will be called Son of God." LUKE 1:35

How do you feel about Christmas, Mary? Does it fill your heart with joy as we celebrate the birth of your son, our Savior, Jesus Christ? Or does it sadden you that so much of the season now comes with a bar code and price tag? Help us to focus on the true reason for the season, dear Blessed Mother Mary. Help us to wait with the same pregnant hope with which you waited for that special day so many years ago.

DECEMBER 13

*[For everything there is a season] a time to tear,
and a time to sew; a time to keep silence, and a time
to speak.* ECCLESIASTES 3:7

This is the season, dear Lord, when I really
have a problem with time. I am running late
for everything from decorating the house to
baking the cookies. And when I get so caught
up in the seasonal demands on my time, I
easily lose sight of what is really important.
Help me today, dear Lord, sometime during the
shopping, decorating and baking to take the
time to be silent, to actually embrace what this
season really means. Help me, please, to make
time for you.

DECEMBER 14

*But now you must get rid of all such things—anger,
wrath, malice, slander, and abusive language from
your mouth.* COLOSSIANS 3:8

Dear God, everyone always thinks of the New
Year as the time to try to clean up their acts.
We wait until January to make our resolution
to be better people. But what better way to
respect the Christmas season than to begin

now to try harder? Today I want to look closely at myself. And when I do, dear Lord, gently show me what it is I need to change. Then give me the grace of working towards that goal as an early Christmas present to others as well as myself.

DECEMBER 15

[I will show] steadfast love to the thousandth generation of those who love me and keep my commandments. EXODUS 20:6

Dear God, we talk so much about how things have changed over the years. With all the inventions of the last hundreds of years, it is not always easy for us to imagine what we have in common with our ancestors. But, Lord, we have you in common with them. What a comfort and what a joy to imagine you loving our ancestors of a thousand years ago, just as you love us now, just as you will love our children's children. Thank you, today for such timeless, endless love.

DECEMBER 16

. . . for in Christ Jesus you are all children of God through faith. GALATIANS 3:26

My dear God, I do love being a parent. Having children has made my life happier, busier, noisier and so much more blessed than ever before. But, nothing compares to being your child, Lord. You are my heavenly Father. And I am your child. Please remind me of that simple and yet essential fact every day of my life. You are my Father. I am your child.

DECEMBER 17

If you sit down, you will not be afraid; when you lie down, your sleep will be sweet. PROVERBS 3:24

Some nights, dear Lord, I do not always get sweet sleep. Many times, there have been little footsteps in the middle of the night followed by a trembling voice that says, "I'm scared. Can I stay with you for awhile?" Help me, Lord, to learn from my children. The next time my sleep is interrupted, not by little footsteps, but by big worries, help me to instinctively know what to do. Help me to turn immediately to you and say, "I'm scared. Can I stay with you for awhile?"

DECEMBER 18

Serve the LORD with fear, with trembling. PSALM 2:11

Dear God, I'm afraid I have never understood
the part about fearing you. I love you! I love
serving you. You are kind and good and gentle.
I just cannot imagine fearing such a loving
Father. Maybe it simply means that I should
always be afraid that I might do something to
make myself fall out of your loving embrace.
I'm not sure. But whatever it means, Lord,
thank you for loving the fear right out of me.

DECEMBER 19

*Blessed are those who trust in the LORD, whose trust
is the LORD.* JEREMIAH 17:7

Have I become a cynic, Lord? Have I become
jaded with doubts and distrust? I don't want to
be that way. Help me to believe again with the
heart of a child. Help me to believe with a
heart that once was capable of believing that
reindeer fly and elves make toys. Help me
believe in you, even when I can't see you near.
Help me, Lord, to trust you. Help me to put all
my trust in you.

DECEMBER 20

A cheerful heart is a good medicine, but a downcast spirit dries up the bones. PROVERBS 17:22

Today, dear Lord, keep me from getting so overwhelmed with my "to-do" list that I become like the bad medicine that dries up the spirit of others around me. Enable me to remain positive even when I am falling behind. Help me, Lord, to have a cheerful heart to give to others during this special season.

DECEMBER 21

Live in harmony with one another. ROMANS 12:16

Dear Lord, I would love for us all to live in harmony, especially now. I mean, is it expecting too much to think I can take my children Christmas shopping without them fighting over who gets to sit in the favorite seat in the minivan? Is it hoping for too much to assume we can bake Christmas cookies together without arguing over who got to put in the most ingredients? Help me, dear Lord, to find more moments of harmony in my house during this precious season of

Christmas. But please remind me not to wish away too soon the precious season of childhood.

December 22

. . . so that my soul may praise you and not be silent. O LORD my God, I will give thanks to you forever. PSALM 30:12

Lord, when my firstborn was a preschooler, she asked me how long forever was. I tried to explain as best as I could what it meant. I told her forever was the length of time I would love her. She replied that she would love me "forever and a day." This is the love I have for my family Lord. This is the love I have for you. I pray that I will be able to show that love and express that love forever—and a day.

DECEMBER 23

"Look, the virgin shall conceive and bear a son, and they shall name him Emmanuel," which means, "God is with us." MATTHEW 1:23

Dear God, thank you for the gift of pregnancy and joyous waiting for a child. It is the gift of hope. At no other time in my life have I felt so closely connected to a miracle in progress. The first flutter, the first kick—words cannot quite express the emotion. Some of my friends who have adopted children and who have waited patiently to care for and love a child of their own tell me of that same expectant hope. Even without a child in their stomach, they feel a flutter and a kick of excitement. Help us all to hold onto those wonderful feelings throughout our lives. Enable us to call up those miraculous moments when we are feeling down and need, perhaps, a little kick just to keep going.

While they were there, the time came for her to deliver her child. And she gave birth to her firstborn son and wrapped him in bands of cloth, and laid him in a manger, because there was no place for them in the inn. LUKE 2:6–7

Dear Mother Mary, I remember being so anxious when my first child was born. I was so frightened of all that was unknown. And I was in a hospital! How did you manage to deliver a baby, the Son of God, in a stable! I wish I could have helped you bring your son into this world, Blessed Mother, but I wasn't there then. Let me be there now. Help me to tell everyone about Jesus. Enable me to help bring your Son into this world today!

December 25
Christmas

But the angel said to them, "Do not be afraid; for see—I am bringing you good news of great joy for all the people: to you is born this day in the city of David a Savior, who is the Messiah, the Lord."
Luke 2:10-11

Dear Lord Jesus, what can I give to you on your birthday? It seems I spend so much of the Christmas season buying gifts for others, but I sometimes forget whose birthday it really is. Forgive me for that. Help me, please, to live today and every day as a gift to you, because you are such a gift to me. Merry Christmas, dear Lord. Happy Birthday!

December 26
Saint Stephen

So they went with haste and found Mary and Joseph, and the child lying in the manger. Luke 2:16

What was going through your mind, dear Mary? What did you think when you held your baby in your arms for the first time? When I first held my baby in my arms, I remember thinking that I was holding the most wonderful child in the world. That baby was more than special to me. How much more intense was that feeling for you, dear Mary? Could you possibly have known what you were truly holding in your arms? Were you at all thinking about the angels, the stars, the Magi? Or were you simply a mother holding and loving her newborn baby?

DECEMBER 27
SAINT JOHN, APOSTLE

In this is love, not that we loved God but that he loved us and sent his Son to be the atoning sacrifice for our sins. 1 JOHN 4:10

Dear Lord, my love for my children has nothing to do with their love for me. I do not change my love for them according to their behavior or attitude. I love them because I love them. Help me please to understand that this is but a brief reflection of your love for your children. Your love is constant and perfect, and yet we have done nothing to deserve it. Your love is just there for us, as you are there for us. Thank you, Lord, for being the perfect example of love.

DECEMBER 28
HOLY FAMILY

Discipline your children while there is hope.
PROVERBS 19:18

On good days, dear Lord, I feel I am right on target with my discipline techniques. I remain calm, collected, firm, but fair. Other days, I am so far off target that no one would believe I was even aiming at all. Please be beside me when I have to discipline my children, Lord. Enable me to be patient and wise. Help me to act instead of simply react. Help me to learn from both the good and bad days.

DECEMBER 29

Therefore encourage one another with these words.
1 THESSALONIANS 4:18

Encouragement. Lord, how we need encouragement! So many days, I will feel my entire spirit physically lifted by a simple phone call or a kind remark. That's all it takes to make a difference in my day. Help me to remember to be that person for others. Grant me the grace of knowing when someone needs a compassionate word or a considerate phone

call. Remind me to make that call today, dear
Lord. Help me to discover the reciprocal grace
of giving.

DECEMBER 30

. . . pray without ceasing. 1 THESSALONIANS 5:17

Dear Lord, some days I suspect no one hears
me when I speak. At times, I wonder if I am
talking to my children or the wall. There surely
seems to be a lot of selective hearing going on
in my house. With this in mind, it is such an
added gift to know that you always listen and
you always hear me. Always. Thank you for
hearing my prayers. Thank you, Lord, for
being the best listener in my life.

DECEMBER 31
NEW YEAR'S EVE

And remember, I am with you always, to the end of the age. MATTHEW 28:20

Thank you, Lord, for being with me throughout this past year. Through the highs and the lows, you were right beside me on this road of motherhood, whether I acknowledged you or not. And thank you for the promise you have given that you will be with me next year, and the year after that, and on and on. I look forward to this journey with you by my side. Thank you, my dear Lord. Amen.